THE SYSTEM

How to Build a Large, Successful Network
Marketing Organization

Don & Nancy Failla

D1316420

sound*concepts*
creative business solutions

Published by
Sound Concepts, Inc.
782 S. Auto Mall Dr. Suite A
American Fork, UT 84003

To Contact Don & Nancy Failla for seminars and conventions, please visit www.45secondtools.com and click on "events."

Original manuscript prepared by Jerry James, DePere, Wisconsin, USA

1st Printing, April 2006
Printed in United States of America

Note: This book was taken from the DVD of our seminar where we teach "The SYSTEM." Other information was written while on a sixteen-day cruise from Beijing, China to Singapore. Sea days were perfect for gathering information.

ISBN 978-1-936631-01-8

10 9 8 7 6 5 4 2 1

Acknowledgments

We would like to thank our kids and grandkids for their love and giving us yet another reason to "Own Our Life." A special thank you to Paul Hirschi and Sound Concepts for helping make this book a possibility and Jerry James for helping us with the original version. We would also like to thank all of those who have used this system and proved that it works!

Our Purpose

The purpose of this book is to teach a person how to instruct others about successfully building their home-based business in a training that will be ten minutes or less. You have not truly started in your new business until you sponsor your first person. The faster you can do this the better off you are.

It is interesting to note that once one learns "The System" there is not much they need to know to make it work. Once you have read this book you will understand why anyone who really wants something can build a business in Network Marketing.

Networking Tools

You very well may have the best "vehicle" in the history of networking (company, products and marketing plan). You may also have the best "gasoline" (motivational CDs, books and other tools). However, if you haven't learned how to duplicate, you simply won't go anywhere.

Knowing what Don and Nancy Failla teach is understanding how to "drive" your vehicle. Once you have studied all the tools Don and Nancy have available, you are not only ready to drive, you're ready for your own personal "Indy 500!" See you at the starting line!

CONTENTS

THE SYSTEM

An Introduction:
Make A Friend, Meet Their Friends

Step 1.
The "45 Second Presentation." Also called "Doing the 45."

Step 2.
Read The 45 Second Presentation book or listen to the audio book version.

Step 3.
Introduce your vehicle: company, products, and compensation plan. The tools are in place. Let them work The System for you!

CHAPTER 1
The Basics Before You Start

Education = Retention

Over the years, I have found that most people involved in network marketing fall into one of the three levels of activity: inactive, frustrated or inspired.

The inactive group are those individuals who were exposed to a network marketing company program but were not interested enough to become involved. Explanations for this state of affairs can range from a poor company presentation to a prospect's negative attitude about the industry in general. Perhaps these people were simply not excited about the product line.

Those people in the frustrated category probably tried network marketing but were unsuccessful. They have remained active because of motivating company meetings, yet lack the ability to get their organization off the ground. Typical causes of frustration are absence of sponsor support, incomplete education about the company program or networking principles and early experiences of rejection.

An inspired individual is the person who will stand the greatest chance of success in network marketing. If you ask a successful network marketing professional what motivates him, he will almost always pinpoint his excitement about the residual income potential of this marketing system as a key factor.

As a result of seeing this over the past 40 years, the advice we give to marketers around the world is learn as much as they can about network marketing and find a company they can believe in! Having a profound knowledge of network marketing not only provides a permanent source of motivation, but also gives them the tools to be successful with almost any company they choose.

Whether you are new or not, start with *The 45 Second Presentation That Will Change Your Life* and seek out other books that will help expand your knowledge about network marketing and how it works.

We wrote *The 45 Second Presentation That Will Change Your Life* 30 years ago because we found ourselves spending literally hours explaining to people what network marketing was and why they should be involved. We quickly realized that spending that much time was counter-productive because: 1 – we explained the same principles over and over and while some prospects were receptive, many were not which wasted our precious time; 2 – our presentations were breaking the cycle of duplication. Not everyone is a dynamic presenter and introducing the business with presentations often scared people away; this is usually exhibited by the prospect with the excuse "I don't have time to do this business.""The System" helps avoid this problem, as we will explain further in the coming chapters.

This is Not a Get-Rich-Quick Business Model

At one time or another, all of us have tried some venture in order to make a quick buck. It's too bad that many people approach network marketing with this mentality because they were led to believe that they could make a lot of money very quickly. This just isn't the way to work in network marketing and it could produce disastrous results. In fact, if you earn big bonus checks in your first month or two, regardless of the program you are in, you may be building your organization like a salesman, or in other words, wrong!

Very large bonuses usually mean that you sponsored too many people in your first line and/or you are "selling" too much product yourself. Directly sponsoring more than five or six serious individuals at at time is an inefficient way to build an organization. It takes depth, not breadth, to realize the benefits of network marketing. Unless you enjoy selling (and therefore stocking and delivering) in a wholesale or retail fashion, concentration on high volume sales will be a real hassle and relatively unprofitable.

It's Not About Who You Know,
It's About Who You Talk To

A common concern from someone just starting (and even some veterans) is that they "don't know who they should approach to grow their organization." The fact is that most people don't realize how many people they already know and or perhaps even more importantly, how many new people they are exposed to or talk to each and every day!

Most people only consider the contacts they you already know. They neglect to present their opportunity to people that they come into contact with each day, including strangers. For those who say "I don't have anyone else to talk to," we say, you're not trying hard enough. Try this simple experiment. Carry a pen and small note pad with you for an entire day and write down the name of every person you talk to either on the phone or in person or any communication with a stranger.

Most people are amazed at how many times they are exposed to potential prospects. There are so many people we see during the day, but that we just don't think about like: postmen, bank tellers, grocery checkers/baggers, gas station attendants, waitresses, receptionists, etc. Now do you believe us?

You don't need to knock on doors or walk up to strangers, cold turkey, and try to "sell" them. But you do need to give others the opportunity to ask you about your business.

How do you get people to ask you about your business? Use human nature to your advantage. When talking with individuals you are not acquainted with, get in the habit of asking what they "do for a living." Showing genuine interest in somebody will undoubtedly cause them to show interest in you and want to know (or at least ask) what you do for a living as well. For those individuals less inclined to start a conversation with others you can deploy another human nature strategy that we find particularly fun and effective.

Without getting into "The System" quite yet, another way you can utilize human nature to start a conversation is to wear the "Own Your Life" lapel pin or other items that may help serve as a conversation starter. People are naturally curious and some may even ask you what the pin means or why you are wearing it. But just as important are the people who see it but don't say anything. If you notice someone looking at your pin or other conversation starter, work up the nerve to say, "I bet you wonder what this means," to get a conversation going.

Employing promotional tools like the lapel pin, business cards, bumper stickers or car decals, shirts and hats draw attention to you and your business. When people see them they are naturally motivated to ask for the meaning of the tool, leading to an opening to start "The System."

CHAPTER 2

The System

The "Pre-Step": Crucial to Success

There are three steps to The System, all of which are discussed at length in the following pages. But there's also a "prestep" that is quite helpful in implementing The System. This crucial prestep is having all the tools necessary to implement The System. Remember these are recommendations based off of our success over the past 43 years and have helped us build our current downline of over 800,000 distributors and growing. However, you may choose to adapt slightly.

Tools Required To Build Using the System:

- A Business Card (or Lifestyle Business Card as we prefer to call them)– this should not have your company name on it and preferably has "The 45 Second Presentation" written on the back for contacts to read. We will talk about why this is important in just a little bit.

- Five to Ten Copies of *The 45 Second Presentation That Will Change Your Life* Book or Audio Book

- Company-Specific Tools – brochures, audio CDs or corporate site that you can refer people to (used in Step 3).

Additional Tools Recommended for Cold Market System:

- IOwnMyLife.net Replicated Website
- Own Your Life lapel pin or similar

THE SYSTEM: STEP 1 –
Giving The 45 Second Presentation

Warm Market

If you go out and immediately start talking about your vehicle (your company, products, marketing plan and so forth), your warm market prospect's first reaction is either going to be that you are just trying to "sell" them something or that they'll need to be a top-notch salesperson to be successful. Because 95 percent of people are non-sales types, you'll get immediate rejections from most prospects. You don't want to blow them away with your vast knowledge of networking or how great your product is, or why your product is better than any other product.

Warm Market vs. Cold Market

The term "warm market" refers to the people you already know. Conversely, the term "cold market" refers to total strangers. A lot of people will say they try to sponsor strangers. However, they don't want to talk to their friends. This group of people has a couple problems. They either don't believe in what they're doing, or they don't understand it. If you believed a person could own their life in one to three years and you understood Network Marketing well enough to explain it in a few minutes—or at least have the book The 45 Second Presentation *explain it for you—why would you want to give this kind of an opportunity to a stranger before your best friend?*

Instead always start with their desire first. To do this you have a conversation with your friends or people you meet about what it would be like if they could own their life.

I recommend you pose a question following lunch with a friend similar to this: "Say, Bill, have you ever thought what it would be like if you could own your life?" There's usually a little pause, because your friend is thinking about the question and is probably not exactly sure what you mean. So you jump in, "You know, Bill, by the time you subtract out the time you spend sleeping, working, commuting, and completing the normal, everyday responsibilities, most people don't own but one or two hours out of every day to do what they'd like to do. And even then, would they have the money to do what they want?"

You continue, "The reason I ask you this question is that I've discovered a way a person can own their life by building a home-based business, and the key is that I have a system that is so simple anybody can do it. It doesn't require selling, and the best part is, it won't take much of your time. Bill, if you're interested, I'll get the first step to you right away."

The 45 Second Presentation is the following phrase used in Step 1 of The System:

This is what I think it means to "own your life"… When you subtract out the sleeping time commuting time, working time and things you have to do each and every day of your life, most people don't have more than one to two hours a day to do what they would like to do; and then, would they have the money to do it?

We have discovered a way a person can learn how to "own their life" by building a home-based business; and we have a system for doing it that is so simple anyone can do it. It doesn't require selling, and the best part is, it won't take much of your time. If you are interested, I can get the first step off to you right away.

CONGRATULATIONS, you just presented "The 45 Second Presentation." Here is how the balance of the conversation in Step 1 should play out.

What does Bill say to you at this point? He might say, "Well gosh, Don, you know I'm not really interested because I'm stuck in a rut. You know, I like going to work to my boring, dead-end job every day." Or he might say, "Sure. I'll take a look. I'm curious to see what you're doing." The key at this point is to be able to end the conversation quickly!

The last part of the this step is to get *The 45 Second Presentation That Will Change Your Life* book or audio book into his hands and ask him to read or listen to the first four chapters. Never, ever tell someone to read the whole book. It will go on the shelf and they will get to it in due time. Having them read the first four chapters is a psychological move. By the time they finish the first four chapters, which goes quickly, most people go on to finish the book.

Excuses: *Avoid Them With "The System"*

The number one "excuse" people have for not doing this business is they say they don't have time. Can you see why someone would say they don't have time after you spend two or three hours in their home, or at an opportunity meeting? Remember, the way you present your opportunity to them is how they think the business must be done. They don't see themselves having the time to spend all those hours doing those lengthy presentations. We have just eliminated that excuse by hardly taking up any of their time.

The number one "reason" people don't do this business is because they don't understand it. After reading The 45 Second Presentation That Will Change Your Life *book, however, they will understand it. At that point we can say, "Now they know how to drive."*

What most people in this business do is start with the vehicle first (company, products, & marketing plan). They spend hours on this and after they sign up they go out and talk to their best prospects and they're crashing and burning all over the place. Why? Because no one taught them how to "drive."

Our philosophy is very simple. We teach people how to drive before we show them the "vehicle." Here is an analogy that really makes this clear.

Let's say you owned a brand new sports car. Would you let your best friend go for a drive around the block if the person did not know how to drive? The sports car is a "hot" vehicle.

In Network Marketing, that's how everyone thinks about their company. It's a "hot" vehicle. They spend hours telling someone about the vehicle. They sign up, go out and crash and burn! That's because nobody taught them how to drive first. Why take a chance that your new person will go out and mess up their best prospects before they even know what they are in? Once they've read the book, however, they will know how to drive.

Cold Market

Another effective gateway to sponsoring is through your cold market. As discussed earlier there are numerous opportunities for you to start conversations with individuals every single day.

Nancy and I always wear a pin that says "Own Your Life." My experience with this has been phenomenal. I've had many, many people approach me and ask, "How do I own my life?"

Once this happens, you respond with, "Before I answer that, let me ask you a question. Do you know anyone who likes to travel or go on a vacation (holiday)?" You're looking for either a "yes" or a "no." Most people will respond, "Yes, I like to." If they say "no" you are finished. Why would you want to sponsor someone who doesn't know anyone that would like to have fun or go on vacation? Notice that you did not ask "them" if they like to travel or go on a vacation (holiday). You used the 3rd person approach and asked them if they "knew anyone."

Because most people will respond favorably to the question, you can simply continue with, "You know it takes three things to travel or go on a vacation. It takes time. It takes money. And it takes good health. If I can show you how you could have all three, would you be interested?"

If you get a "no" you are finished. Isn't it exciting to know this after only a few seconds rather than spending two or three hours doing an in-home or opportunity meeting presentation?

Next you ask, "Tell me, what would it mean to you to be able to own your life?" This is both the most difficult as well as the easiest part of this conversation. It's easy because there's no dialogue to learn. It's difficult because you have to shut up and let them talk. For most sales types, that's typically a hard thing to do.

Understand that the more they talk, the better prospect you have. When I ask this question at sizzle sessions (these are explained later), I go around the table and ask each person. You can ask your friend the question, "What would you do with your life if you owned it?"

If the person thinks it over and then says that he or she really doesn't know, you could ask, "Okay, great. Do you like to travel?" If they say they don't care, then it's readily apparent they probably aren't a good prospect.

It's important to remember that it doesn't matter what a person wants—a bigger home, a boat, a plane, an automobile, or other material things. Maybe they'd like more available time for their family, community service, church work, or politics. Whatever it is the person wants can be acquired by involvement in this business. The point is this—if the person doesn't desire anything, you simply don't have a prospect. Even if they did eventually enroll, it would more than likely be as a wholesale buyer, or to simply get you off their back. But they will not become an active business builder. Therefore, you must let them talk first.

More On Time, Money And Health

How many people do you know who have all three? How many people do you know who would like to have all three? Young people who are working might have money and good health. However, they don't have time. Older people who are retired have time. However, they may be short of money. They cannot go and visit their grandchildren any time they want. Or they know they're getting older—so what about their health?

When you are successful in Network Marketing, you could have all three: time, money and health in one to three years. It is a great life when you can do whatever you want, whenever you want, and with whomever you choose.

After they finish responding to your question, you say, "Well, what I think it means is that by the time you subtract out the sleeping time, commuting time, working time, and all the things you have to do each and every day of your life, most people don't own but one to two hours a day of their life . . ."

By now, you're into the conversation only a minute or two.

Once you get to this point, hand them your lifestyle business card with your IOwnMyLife.net or other lifestyle site address on it. Tell them to check out the website online and when they are ready to take a serious look, to fill out the survey online and you will get back with them. This step is important. At this point you have just met this person. You know nothing about them.

The IOwnMyLife.net replicated site acts as a sift and sort tool for your cold market. You send people to the site, they can watch the first couple napkin presentations and read a little bit more about "Lifestyle Training" and fill out the survey to get more info from you. The survey is the perfect way for you to become more acquainted with their objectives and commitment level converting your cold market contacts to your warm market prospects. After they have filled out the survey you now have a better relationship established than you did when you first met and are better poised to help them achieve the goal of "owning their life."

Why Step 1 Works

When I conduct seminars, I ask the attendees, "How many people here would like to own more of their life? To have the time, money and health to do whatever you would like to do?" Just from spontaneity, everybody in the room usually raises their hand.

Let me explain why I believe this approach is so powerful. It's powerful because, in the first place, most people do not own very much of their lives. They not only don't own very much of their lives, but they don't even realize it. They are so busy trying to make a living and make ends meet, they haven't stopped to contemplate the fact they have practically no free time to call their own.

When you use this analogy, it's like putting a little stone in a person's shoe. Have you ever had a stone in your shoe? You keep walking and you think it's going to go away, but it never really does. Sooner or later you're going to have to do something about it, right?

Well, the thing about putting this little stone in a person's shoe is that it has the ability to grow. They go to work and have a bad day on their job. The boss gets on their case. That stone just got a little bit bigger. Or when their kid says, "Hey, Dad, our team is going out of town next week for a special ball game. Can you come?"

And Dad has to reply, "Gee, son, I'm sorry. I can't go because I have to go to work." That stone just got a little bigger. The point here, again, is that once you've introduced this whole concept, you've planted a stone that can only grow.

The key in this approach is that once the person gets to the point where he or she says, "You know, I've got to do something about this stone in my shoe," the only thing they can do that would make any sense at all is get involved in a home-based business in Network Marketing. For the masses, there is no other answer.

What if someone were to say, "Come on, Don, I could win the lottery." I'd ask them if they bought a ticket that week. Besides, have you ever seen what happens to people who win the lottery? In three to five years they're worse off than before they won, according to surveys. What about the guy three years ago who won $3.6 million, and after two weeks of being harassed by his friends to borrow money, became so stressed out he died of a heart attack?

It's true that you could own your business outside of Network Marketing. Some of you may already own one, or know people who do. But the truth is, doesn't the business own you? You don't really own the business. For instance, my wife, Nancy, and I owned an International House Of Pancakes many years ago. We operated it for four years. During that period we only got three full days off. We were open 24 hours a day, 7 days a week, and we employed 35 teenagers. It was a nightmare. So we know what it means not to own virtually any of our lives.

At one seminar a couple of years ago, with about 300 people in attendance, I asked everyone who had a substantial inheritance coming to raise their hands nice and high. What would you expect out of 300 people? There were six people who raised their hands. I said to the rest of them, "How would you like to be in their shoes? Where you have to wait 10, 20 or perhaps 30 years for the person to die? And, frankly, some of them will probably outlive you anyway." The crowd had a good laugh.

There are few things in life that are 100 percent guaranteed. Two things we know for sure: we were all born, and someday we're all going to die. However, there's a third thing that is 100 percent guaranteed. If you're an employee or if you have friends who are employees, neither you nor they will ever own very much of your lives unless you get involved in your own home-based business in Network Marketing.

So, basically, this is a very strong approach—the "Own Your Life" approach. When you ask a person if they'd like to "own their life" and the person's reply is actually telling you, "No, thanks. I'm happy in my rut. I like going to my boring, dead-end job," then you're done with that prospect. And you wasted only about 30 seconds of your own time.

Understand that if I thought I was going to be in for a two- to five-hour presentation every time I introduced the concept of Network Marketing to a prospect, I would have been burned out a long time ago. How many of those lengthy presentations can you do anyway? I'm into this thing for about 30 seconds inquiry time. Then I get out of it. I let the tools take over. The tools do the bulk of the work in this approach.

Here's a brief story to sum up this section. Not too long ago, Nancy and I had breakfast with a friend named Mac. We hadn't seen Mac for many years. Needless to say, Mac was totally overwhelmed by our possessions and our lifestyle. We had just returned from a cruise, and in another three months we were going on a sixteen-day cruise through the Panama Canal. We'd also just bought our boys a brand new, super-loaded, red Corvette. All of this totally blew Mac's mind. He couldn't handle the suspense any longer, so he finally asked me, "Okay, Don. Tell me—what are you selling?"

My answer to Mac is the ultimate key to understanding how to build your business in the easiest and fastest manner. I told him, "Mac, what we are selling is your life. We sell you the opportunity to own your own life. Network Marketing is the only realistic answer."

Step #2: *Reading (or Listening to)* The 45 Second Presentation That Will Change Your Life *Book*

The second step in The System is to understand Network Marketing and how to drive or, in other words, knowing how to succeed in this business. People who don't understand what we're teaching have a tendency to go directly from building desire ("Own Your Life") in the first step, to the "vehicle" (talking about the company, products, marketing plan, and so forth). Let me explain why that's a major mistake.

Let's say you owned a car lot in your city, but nobody within 300 miles knew how to drive. How many cars are you going to move? Probably none. So what should you do? You should set up a driving school and teach people how to drive. Once they know how to drive, then they'll want a car. Another way to put it is like this: let's say that I give you a Lamborghini tomorrow, which is a hot car. If you don't know how to drive it, then you're not going to go anywhere. The vehicle is capable of taking you any place you'd ever want to go, provided you know how to drive.

People in our industry sometimes jump from one vehicle to the next vehicle to still another always looking for the newest "hot" deal. The reason they don't achieve success in any one of them is because they never knew how to drive the first one. You've got to know how to drive. You can learn how to drive then, essentially, by understanding the Ten Napkin Presentations. These are explained in detail in my book, *The 45 Second Presentation That Will Change Your Life.*

So, in Step 2, we offer a prospect the book I just mentioned. By the time a person goes through and understands the Ten Napkin Presentations, they'll understand that they can build a business without being a salesperson. They'll understand, too, that anybody they know can build a huge business if they'd only get involved for five to ten hours a week for six months in order to learn how to do it.

How do you get your friends to read the book? It goes back the analogy that I used about the stone in the shoe. You do step 1 and they may not be ready, and that is fine. Let that stone fester; don't force it. Otherwise if they are ready loan them the book and ask them to read the first four chapters. Again, this is a psychological move; once they start, they will finish the book.

I've seen many people give the first step to a prospect on one day, and the prospect got so excited they were immediately ready for the second step. Be prepared to be able to follow through with The System by having the tools on hand.

In order to explain Network Marketing properly to someone, it would take you from three to four hours to teach them the Ten Napkin Presentations. We don't teach it that way any longer. At a seminar, I illustrate what I mean like this: I stand in front of three people, as I step in front of each person, I explain that it takes me three to four hours to explain Network Marketing to this person, then another three to four hours to explain it to this one, then another three to four hours to explain it to this third individual as well. That would require from nine to twelve hours of explaining! Then I step back in front of each one again and I introduce them to "The 45 Second Presentation" and *The 45 Second Presentation That Will Change Your Life* book—all of which takes only one minute!

The reason we offer to loan them the book or the audio book is that we don't know which way the person prefers to learn. But we do know that if they read the book or listen to the audio version, they've gone through the material and it will become totally clear to them why they and most anyone they know can build a huge business in Network Marketing.

By standing in front of these people the second time and explaining that it takes only one minute to loan the first one the presentation and book, then one minute to loan the second the presentation and book, and likewise one minute for the third person—I make my point clear. I say, "You know, this almost sounds crazy, but we say it's better to spend three minutes with three people than nine to twelve hours!" Of course, everybody totally relates to that.

After a prospect has completed the second step, they're going to come back to you and say something like, "Boy, I don't own my life. But I want to. I understand the basics of Network Marketing now. What's next?"

The System Step #3: *Presenting The "Vehicle"*

Finally, I'm going to teach you how to introduce your vehicle. And again, you can do this without really knowing much.

Before starting, let me explain that by "vehicle," I'm referring to the company, products and compensation plan for which you're a distributor. When it comes to the "vehicle," just about everybody thinks that theirs is the hot vehicle.

Here's a common scenario. You go over to a friend's house and you spend two or three hours telling them about your hot "vehicle." They get excited. They jump in. Then they go out and start talking to all their friends before they even know what they are doing. They don't even understand this business yet. Pretty soon they are crashing and burning all over the place!

Like I said before, if you had a really "hot" car, such as a Lamboghini, would you let your best friend go for a drive around the block in your brand new car if they did not know how to drive?

Why, then, would you show your friend your hot vehicle (new company and product) and let them go out and talk to people before they even understand how to drive the car (Network Marketing)? It's a disaster waiting to happen. Instead, before we ever even show them our vehicle, we first need to teach them how to drive.

And what is the best way to present your "vehicle"? Well, that depends on you. There are meetings, party plans, and the like. There's the one-on-one meeting. And there are also tools—such as booklets, audio CDs, video DVDs, newsletters, websites and so on—that really do a great job of explaining your vehicle.

These tools have made it very easy to explain to prospects on the vehicle and get them excited about it. This is especially true if you have done an effective job in Steps 1 and 2. If they are comfortable with these concepts, then they will find that introducing the vehicle (company or product), especially with the help of professionally produced educational tools, is not difficult. And you're there to *take care of* any questions they might have.

However, as good as CDs or websites may be at introducing a company or product, I believe that the most important tool in promoting your vehicle is your sponsor. This brings me to one more important point. Notice that in the previous paragraph, I said "take care of" instead of "answer" the questions. How can you answer specific questions about a product when you don't know much about your product yet? How do you "take care" of them? It's easy! You simply call them, tell them you have your sponsor, Don, on the phone. And Don is going to "answer the questions on my behalf—while I listen in—because that is how I learn."

That is a powerful phrase, "This is how I learn." So, what did you have to know in order to explain your vehicle? Well, after getting your prospect through Steps 1 and 2, you only had to have your sponsor participate on a three-way call. That summarizes the whole business. Pretty simple, right? Here's another way to introduce the vehicle using your sponsor. Let's say you, your sponsor and your prospect all live in the same area. You invite both of them to lunch with the understanding that after the meal, your sponsor is going to explain the vehicle on your behalf.

During the meal, you simply don't talk about the vehicle. Instead, you're only going to discuss the prospect—their family, their interests, where they live, their goals and aspirations, what they would like to do if they "owned their life," etc. The more we get the prospect talking, the better prospect we have.

After the meal is over, your sponsor would then explain the vehicle to your prospect. And keep it short! In my opinion, it is not wise to spend more than about 15 minutes talking about the products, company and compensation plan. Never go more than 20 minutes with a prospect! After they sign up, you can go spend more time with them to make sure they understand.

Again, what they see you doing is what they think they will have to do to be successful. If you're spending hours of time on each individual prospect, they will believe they have to do the same, and there's a good chance you'll lose them.

So, remember that it is important to learn to "not talk." Talking is our worst enemy. We have to learn to talk just enough, then let the tools do the instructing for you. The more you talk to your prospect, the more he or she will begin to think that they can't or don't want to do what you're doing.

What Could Be More Simple?

You can see that with these steps—The System—we have eliminated the weekly opportunity meeting. And we don't need to have in-home or one-on-one presentations. All we have to do is introduce the "own your life" concept, either locally or long distance, get them started with the three steps and follow through The System. It's so simple. Anyone can do it. You can learn The System in less than 10 minutes and teach it in less than 10 minutes. Now that's duplication! Remember, the easier it is to duplicate, the more people will succeed, and the faster your business will grow!

THE SYSTEM

STEP 1 –

Warm Market
- Present The 45 Second Presentation

Cold Market
- Present the 45 Second Presentation using your Lifestyle Business Card with The 45 Second Presentation printed on the back.
- Refer them to your IOwnMyLife.net site, also printed on your card, to take the survey.

STEP 2 – Loan them *The 45 Second Presentation That Will Change Your Life* book and ask them to read the first four chapters.

STEP 3 – Present your vehicle using your sponsor or company tools like brochures, CDs, DVDs, or company site.

CHAPTER 3
Long-Distance Sponsoring Made Simple

What's the best way to sponsor long distance? You have to use The System. The same principles taught in the previous chapter can be applied locally and over long distances. With The System, you can actually introduce the concept of Network Marketing to a person 2,500 miles away in no more than a couple of minutes on your IOwnMyLife.net site or over the phone. That would be your total talking time or time spent sending a presentation from your site to them.

When you sponsor people nowadays, chances are those people have come from another community, even if you sponsored them locally. So their best prospects are really where they came from before you met them—that is, the place where they spent their childhood or lived most of their life. Maybe you have just moved to your current residence, or have lived in your current community for a year or two. If so, your new neighbors aren't typically your best prospects. Who is? Those individuals you've known all your life.

When first getting started, most people in the networking industry don't know how to effectively work a system or how to sponsor someone long-distance. New distributors are usually taught to build their businesses locally first. Of course, to build a business locally, there are three things that people typically do: 1) hold opportunity meetings, 2) host in-home presentations, and/or 3) arrange for one-on-one presentations. Although they may help you locally, those three things will not help you sponsor at long distances. It's virtually impossible to do those things 2,500 miles from your home base.

Therefore, what we teach people to use The System to sponsor and teach long-distance. Once you know The System you can then use the same technique with someone 2,500 miles away, 25 miles away, 5 miles away, or right across the street.

This is important because it means that when you sponsor new people, they have the opportunity of working with their best prospects from the time they become active. Most people get involved in Network Marketing and fail in the business before they ever have the chance to get to their best prospects.

The System (and its tools) will literally do the work for you. Introduction to the steps within The System may only take one or two minutes. Consequently, you'll save hours of long distance telephone conversations. Now just let The System work for you.

Long-Distance Support *(Sponsoring by Phone / Skype & Creating National Sizzle Sessions)*

Now you've sponsored someone and they are 2,500 miles away. How do you support them? First of all, you do it by communicating with them on the phone or skype periodically. You keep in touch to help them stay motivated, and to help them sponsor others. How do you help them sponsor by long distance? By what is known as "two-on-one."

In other words, when you have someone who has a prospect they're trying to sponsor at a distance, and they get to Step 3 of The System, they will probably need some help. And you're the one to provide it.

First, you can set up a three-way conference call. That way, you can help your new person by talking to the person they're trying to sponsor. This is very supportive. All they have to do is be quiet and let you do the talking. It's an ideal way for them to learn.

Skype: *Another Useful Tool*

The latest method of communicating is Skype. What is it? While it's not Network Marketing, it is free and it can be a big help in building your networking business. It's just like having free long distance but instead of telephone, you talk via your home computer using a microphone or headset.

To enroll, go to www.skype.com. It only takes about two minutes to register and then you can talk on Skype to anywhere in the world to anyone who is also on the Skype network. It's a marvelous service.

Along this same idea, we have groups that do conference calling. When you set up a conference call, you can have unlimited numbers of people on the line. For example, let's say you set it for Wednesday evening at 8 o'clock. You put the word out to all of your people that you're going to have a conference call with some training and support at that specific time and date. You get the phone number out to all of your people.

Now, there are different ways of doing this. You can set it up where everybody gets to talk. Or when your group becomes large enough (or too large to have everybody talking at once), you can set it up where only maybe four people are doing the talking while the rest are simply listening.

You can also expand by going to a toll-free number, where everybody would call in. But then, of course, you end up paying for all the calls. I don't normally suggest that you alone bear all the burden of the expense. On these kinds of setups, I would recommend that you keep the time allotted to around 15 to 20 minutes. Short and sweet. It's just to give people a chance to touch base on a weekly basis. It gives people an opportunity to experience some real enthusiasm and become re-energized.

Create National Sizzle Sessions

The other thing you do as soon as your new long-distance distributor sponsors their first person locally is to tell them to set up a local "sizzle session." The sizzle session is explained in detail in Napkin Presentation #8 in my book, *The 45 Second Presentation That Will Change Your Life*. As a brief review, a sizzle session is getting two or more people together to share ideas about what it is they're doing. We use the analogy that if you had a campfire and you had one log, it's like sitting in a restaurant by yourself. You virtually have nothing. No energy, no feedback, no enthusiasm. But when you have two logs, you can have a flame. If you combine three you can create a fire. When there are four or more together, then you have a real blaze! As the number of people increase at your sizzle sessions, the more energy and communication flow you have.

We used to have a sizzle session every Wednesday evening from 6 to 9 pm in Las Vegas. We were up to 40 people that were coming and going. I need to make it very clear that a sizzle session is not an opportunity meeting. This is not a place where a person would send or bring a prospect to hear about an opportunity. A sizzle session is for people already enrolled in the business to come and share ideas and get their questions answered on how to do the business. A sizzle session is not one person putting on a 45 minute or an hour presentation to the rest of the people there. Instead, everyone gets to discuss and exchange ideas. This creates a fun atmosphere.

It's kind of interesting to note that in many of our sizzle sessions, only 15 to 30 minutes of the entire 2-hour block was used to actually talk about the vehicle. Instead, the first thing we usually did when we started our sizzle sessions was to talk about fun things. Things like the "unconventions" that were coming up.

You may wonder what an unconvention is. Well, when you go to a convention it's usually at a beautiful resort. However, you're in meetings all day, so you don't get to enjoy the facilities. And there's something very interesting that typically happens at conventions. Have you noticed that you always learn the most during the breaks, sharing ideas with successful people?

The general idea to an unconvention is that there are no meetings. The whole thing is one big break from the time people get there until everyone leaves. It's one big get-together out by the swimming pool from about 10 am until 5 pm every day. People literally come from all over the world, all different Network Marketing companies. We just sit around the pool, have fun, and share ideas. You can go out to dinner with people you might have just met from Australia. During the day, we all decide which one of the many shows available we want to go to in the evening. If you choose to, that is. Some join the group. Others do their own thing.

We also talk about our unconvention cruises, or come up with other ideas about things to do to have fun while you're building a business. The whole idea of the fast way to build your business is that you build it by having fun. People like to associate and belong to a fun group. And if you're having fun, they're going to want to join you. Remember, as we teach in Napkin Presentation #8 about sizzle sessions, be aware of the person who's overhearing your conversations.

We even have sizzle sessions at bowling alleys. We bowl one or two lanes, then go into the coffee shop for an hour or so and share ideas. We've also had one just recently on a sixty-foot sailboat in Miami in Biscayne Bay. It was great. Again, we try to share ideas and information while having a good time. You can be very creative about when and where you have sizzle sessions.

Here are some tips on scheduling sizzle sessions. First, if you're having a lunch-time session on a weekday, I would recommend that you schedule it at about 1:15 pm in a restaurant of your choice. Keep it at a middle-of-the-road type of restaurant. We've also had them in buffet courts where we just take over a whole section and everybody can just go and get whatever they want. You don't want to start it at noon because it's too crowded and noisy, there's too much smoke, and everybody's in a big hurry during the lunch rush. If you start at 1:15, by the time you get through with your lunch, the restaurant has usually cleared out somewhat, leaving you with a little more space and a bit less noise.

Also, when you arrive at the restaurant, let the waitress know that you tip by the hour. So that when you're there a little bit longer than normal, they don't become stressed out thinking they're going to lose a lot of tips because their tables aren't turning.

And regarding smoking, we respect that it's a person's choice. But at the same time, for those non-smokers, we do not allow smoking in the immediate proximity of our sizzle sessions. If a person wants to smoke, they understand that they should go outside. If you allow just one person to smoke at your sizzle sessions, and you have a new person there sitting next to the smoker, you might end up never seeing this new prospect again because they may get the impression that every time they come to a sizzle session they've got to endure inhaling someone's cigarette smoke. A little courtesy is all that's necessary.

When we do sizzle sessions at a pool, restaurant or on our boat, we like to pose the question, "So how do you like our new office facility?" That's because we don't have a fixed office, other than a little office in our home. Our offices are the resorts and restaurants of the world. In these venues, we can enjoy a beautiful atmosphere and associate with people who want more out of life.

Let's now talk a bit about how to expand a local sizzle session into a national calendar of sizzle sessions.

National Calendar Of Sizzle Sessions

When you first begin building your business, you're going to network with both your upline and downline. Encourage as many people as you can to arrange a sizzle session in their area. There are cities that are large enough where you could have twenty-five sizzle sessions going on in the same week. Take a city like Chicago, for example. You could have sizzle sessions at the north end of town, the south end of the town, and the west end of the town. If you have one on the east end of town, you'd better have a boat because you would be out in the middle of Lake Michigan.

You could have them in the afternoon. You could have them in the evening. You could have them late at night. For example, in Las Vegas, Lake Tahoe, Atlantic City, and other places like this, you could actually have a sizzle session that starts at 4 am because a lot of these people get off late at night and that's the only time they could attend a sizzle session.

There are no definite rules as to when you can or can't have them. Just try to avoid extremely busy times in a restaurant. You should be aware of that. Also be aware that waiters and waitresses make their living from tips, so be generous when tipping these people. They overhear bits and pieces of your conversation, and they're curious about what you're doing. They get the feeling this is a group that's going someplace. And if you don't leave a tip, or leave a small tip, that's not too exciting for them. As a general rule, if I'm responsible for organizing the sizzle session, I encourage everyone to be sure and leave a nice tip. I also seek out the waiter or waitress before leaving and give them an extra $5 bill (or $10, depending on the size of the group).

Also, when you arrive at your location, make sure it is clear with the waitress that you need separate checks. Everyone is in business for themselves, and they can write off meals when they're out working their business, so they're all going to need separate checks for their own write-off. No one person wants to be responsible for the expense of the entire group. It's much better for each individual to take care of his or her own checks.

We are in the process of getting as many people to hold a weekly sizzle session as they can (and we encourage anyone with any company to do the same). And then organize this into a national calendar of sizzle sessions. Could you imagine if we had two to four hundred locations in all the major cities all over the country where there were sizzle sessions going on each week? You could call a friend, say for example, in Denver. You've got them started on track with The System. You've got them through Step 3. They've sent their application in. You can tell the new distributor now, "You know what you should do now, Bill. Tuesday evening go down to Denny's at such-and-such a location at 7 o'clock. Ask the hostess where the sizzle session is. She can direct you to the people there." This way, your new person gets a chance to meet with other people working the business in their area so they can share ideas and get their questions answered.

Now, I want to make something absolutely clear. Do not send a prospect to an out-of-town sizzle session before they are signed up in your program. You don't want to give someone else the responsibility of explaining everything to your person. That's not the purpose of the sizzle session.

Besides, you are this person's friend. It's risky because if you get them started on The System, but they still haven't signed up, they may end up meeting at that sizzle session their second best friend. And the second best friend says, "You mean you haven't signed up yet? Well, gosh, I'm right here. Why don't you let me sponsor you?" You see, you don't want someone to lose a prospect to that kind of situation.

If you want to bring a prospect to your own local sizzle session, that is okay. But again, I would do that on the condition that before you bring the person to the sizzle session, they have gone through the first two steps. Otherwise, they may be so uninformed that they begin asking so many fundamental questions, which will take up people's time reviewing concepts that they could have easily read from the book. We say that really there are no dumb questions, but the bottom line is that any question that could have been answered by the person going through the first two steps prior to coming to the sizzle session is a foolish question.

Could you imagine being able to sit down with a your new prospect and showing them your calendar of sizzle sessions around the country? You'll get to explain to them, "Now here's how this works. You contact your friends out of town. See if they'd like to own their life. If they're interested, you send them the first step, the second step, and you get their commitment. You send them the vehicle. Now you send them to a local sizzle session. And of course, they can do the same. This is a huge opportunity for you to not only sponsor at a distance, but give them to local support teams virtually all over the country."

Telephone Your Way To Success:
Conference Calling Support For Network Marketers

It's no secret that person-to-person communications is the essence of Network Marketing. The very concept of Network Marketing is based upon leveraging an individual's personal sphere of influence, i.e., "If I know five people who know five people…" and so on. But what if those acquaintances are located in another city, another state, or even in a foreign country? The challenge is obviously how to excite and engage someone about your lifestyle, company or product when a physical, face-to-face meeting isn't always possible.

The solution? A conference call. As Network Marketers, you'll discover that teleconferencing—the linking of groups of people over the telephone lines—meets this challenge with an efficiency and effectiveness never before available. Let's take an inside look at how conference calling works, how it can be used to grow your organization, and how it can actually generate revenues for you.

Nancy Failla on Sizzle Sessions

Sizzle sessions are the fun way to build your Network Marketing business. I always tell people that if they're going to build an organization, why not build it the fun way? Sizzle sessions are definitely fun!

A sizzle session is an enjoyable and educational social event. This is not where you're going to solve the world's problems or discuss all the problems in your life. This is a very social function. I like to tell people that if you know a lot of lonely people, why don't you start a sizzle session? You can share your ideas for the business, as well as plan some fun things, like potlucks, bowling parties, picnics, or "unconventions." We've had sizzle sessions on cruise ships. We've had them in motor homes and in trailers. You can have them on your lunch hour at work, or in your home. We've even had them standing in a parking lot!

As you know, our motto is "Own Your Life." That means you can have the time, money and health to be able to whatever you want with your life. And remember, you could build all this around sizzle sessions. The sessions become more and more exciting as time goes on. They get easier and easier as well. You will find that your sizzle sessions will grow because everybody wants to be with a fun, social group. Let's face it. These are the movers and shakers of the world. These are the people who realize there really is a better way to a better life. So let's get on with it and start having more fun.

To hold an opportunity meeting, you would typically book a room at a local hotel. In the case of a conference call, the hotel is replaced by a "bridge" (a computer which accommodates a large number of incoming phone lines). The bridge can be segmented into a number of telephone meetings, depending upon the size of your call.

Long-Distance Sizzles And More

Although the most common type of conference call is a large, motivational session conducted for recruiting purposes, other types of calls are also used by Network Marketers. Following is an overview of the most typical applications:

• Interactive Calls, where all participants can converse freely with each other. These calls are particularly suited to groups of 20 or fewer.

• Speaker/Audience Calls, which have a limited number of interactive lines and a virtually unlimited number of active lines. These calls are great for training sessions and newscasts to update distributor networks. Most commonly, they are used for recruiting new distributors in a downline organization.

• Parent/Subordinate Calls, which are actually Speaker/Audience calls with a number of smaller conferences linked in for listening purposes. An advantage is that costs are distributed among many hosts, each of whom pays for their own recruits.

• Pre-Recorded and Rebroadcast Calls, which are appropriate for individuals who were unable to attend the original presentation. Pre-recording is also an excellent solution when a guest speaker is unavailable for live conference.

Consider These Benefits Of Conference Calling

• *You can attract the most desirable, sought-after speakers. If they're not available for live participation on the call, it's a snap to pre-record their message and play it directly into a conference call.*

• *Geographic limitations no longer exist. Conference calls span three or four time zones and can accommodate hundreds of participants.*

• *Calls can be booked at the last minute, with very little preparations. You can get your news into the hands of the people that need it while it's still hot!*

Summary: *Conference Calls Can Be Used For...*

• Long-distance sponsoring
• Long-distance training
• Long-distance support
• Long-distance leadership meetings

… and other events that used to require hotel and travel expenses, time away from business, scheduling conflicts and all the other headaches of personal presentations and support.

Conference-calling customers—from first-time distributors to seasoned veterans—make more money and have more time to enjoy it. Isn't that exactly why you're in Network Marketing?

CHAPTER 4
Using Your Upline & Investing In Your Business

In this chapter, I discuss two things that, if you learn to take advantage of them, will help you build your business more quickly and effectively. So read ahead to find out how your upline and investing a few dollars in distributing *The 45 Second Presentation That Will Change Your Life* book will make a huge difference for you.

Making Use Of Your Upline, Your Best Tool

The first thing you want to do with every new distributor is send them a list of the names, addresses and phone numbers of all the people in their upline from five to seven levels above them. Instruct them that after they've "gotten their feet wet" (meaning they've reviewed their distributor kit, begun using the products, and are ready to get busy building their business, etc.), they should start at the bottom of their upline list and call everyone in their upline. After introducing themselves, they should say why they're excited to be in the business, and ask if the upline distributor has anything they can send to help them get their business kick-started.

It's kind of exciting because this is a way of motivating the upline. And when that new person sponsors someone, they should do this same thing, too. Eventually you're going to start getting a lot of phone calls. It's pretty exciting to be sitting at home and your phone rings and the conversation can go something like this, "Hi, Don. You don't know me, but my name is John. I'm from Houston, and I'm in your downline." "Hey, no kidding. Isn't that neat?" You see, you are going to be excited because you just got a call from a brand new distributor. I don't care how long you've been in this business; there will never be anything that will excite you more than knowing that someone in your downline is motivated to get rolling.

The more people you sponsor, the more people who will send out this upline list, and the more your name is on the upline, before long you could be getting two or three calls a day. Soon you could be getting five to ten calls a day. You don't mind. The more calls you get the better. You enjoy talking to these people. All you have to do is let them know that any time they have anyone that you could talk to and help support on their behalf, you'll be glad to. But only under one condition—that the new prospect has already completed Steps 1 and 2 before you call them. You see, they are their friends and prospects, so they should supply a copy of *The 45 Second Presentation That Will Change Your Life* to their friend first. If they put you in touch with these people before they've taken them through the first two steps, you might be stuck on a long-distance call for several hours explaining everything, which is totally unnecessary because the tools should have done all the work prior to that.

Here's another advantage to contacting and working with your upline. Imagine this scenario. Let's say I'm talking to John from Houston. I say, "John, you know, I know some people who live in the Houston area who are not really self-starters. I was hoping to find someone like you that's serious about building a business in that area so I can contact these people. I'll go ahead and call them. I'll get them through the first two steps. Then when they're ready for the vehicle, and they need some more information, I'll refer these prospects to you. You can go ahead and get together with them on my behalf. Then you can go ahead and sponsor them yourself."

There are a lot of interesting things that can happen when you get people communicating upline and downline. If your new person makes five to seven calls to their upline, then obviously they're going to become very motivated as they contact each one. Then, the following week, they'll be motivated once again as they start receiving packages from these different people in the upline. This is really a strong way to motivate a new person who's trying to get started.

Investing In Your Business: *Using The* 45 Second *Book For Bigger, Better Growth*

When we personally sponsor someone the first thing we do is send them five copies of *The 45 Second Presentation That Will Change Your Life*. Beyond this, we send out a book to each new person coming into the downline to unlimited levels.

When a new person is sponsored and has gone on Auto Ship (an automatic monthly order), they need to email us the person's name, address, phone number and email address. We then send them a complimentary book. We do this for the person we sponsor all the way down the line until they get to a certain level in the marketing plan. This is a level where they are now making good money. If they want to continue with the giveaway program, they are now on their own for getting books to their downline.

So again, we say, "Better to spend a few dollars and involve yourself in a two-minute or less conversation with a friend or a person you meet, than to get together with them and spend two to five hours." In the case of the long distance, how are you going to get together with them?

Whether you are in a stair-step, break-away, or matrix-style marketing plan, it doesn't matter. You should get together with your leaders and determine what it is worth when you sponsor a person and they reach certain levels of achievement with your program. Usually, I like to figure out a level that would return a thousand dollars a month to me. Then another level where this person could be worth two to four thousand dollars a month. If you determine, then, that once this new person has achieved this level where they're worth a thousand dollars a month to you, how many investments in books, DVDs, and other tools would you be willing to spend to be able to locate that person who could be worth a thousand dollars or more per month to you? That's how investing pays off.

Every program is different. You must determine the different levels, what the value is, and what it's worth to you to find that new person. You should also look at the burnout factor. Nancy and I have been in this industry going on thirty-nine years. If I thought that every time I introduced the concept of Network Marketing to someone, I was in for a two-to five-hour ordeal with them, I would have been burned out years ago. But I am more excited about this industry today than I've ever been because I know that I can meet with a person and introduce the concept and check their desire level very quickly.

Let me give you an example. I'm sitting in a jacuzzi. We're visiting with someone else sitting in the jacuzzi. I ask them what they do. Remember, when you ask someone what they do, nine out of ten people will ask you what you do. If you tell them that you sell something, and that person is a non-sales type, you are finished before you get started. But if you will do what Nancy and I do, then you've got a shot. When the person asks me what I do for a living, I say, "Well, my wife and I are Lifestyle Trainers. We teach people how to own their life."

At this point, they look a little puzzled. So then I go on and say, "By the time you subtract out the sleeping time, commuting time… [the same explanation as before]. We have developed a way you can own your life by building a home-based business. And we have a system that is so simple, anybody can do it. You don't have to be a salesperson and it doesn't require much of your time. If you're interested, give me your card before you leave, I'll send the first step out to you right away." Now, there you are, you've gotten yourself in motion with a new person, and it took very little time.

I keep mentioning the word "System." Let me tell you a little story. There was a man named Ray Kroc who bought a company called McDonald's. He didn't buy McDonald's to sell hamburgers. He bought it because it was a money machine that was easy to duplicate. The net result was people bought hamburgers. So far, billions of burgers.

We did not get involved in the company we're working to sell their products. The company is a money machine. With our System, it's easy to duplicate. The net result is, people will buy the company's products. Now, as an interesting afterthought, when you tell someone this little story, you simply ask, "What if Ray Kroc was a vegetarian?" It really doesn't make any difference—he wasn't in it for the product, but more for the strength of the business model.

At this point I would like to clarify our position on retailing in Network Marketing. We teach that to make the big checks—which for most people would be from two to five thousand a month (and for others that means 10, even 50 thousand or more per month)—you do that by building a large organization. People don't make those big checks from merely retailing products. Retailing has an important place. Basically, its place is in the process of building your organization. When we show the 5, 25, 125 growth at subsequent levels, we say that is like building a pipeline. As you build the pipeline (organization), the products will naturally flow through it.

For instance, if people say no to the opportunity, you share some product samples with them, and you get them to become what we call "friend customers." So if everybody in the process of building their business ends up with 10 friend customers, this is where the retailing is involved in Network Marketing.

It's just a simple shift in attitude. You will get retail customers in the process of building your business. You don't go out and get a large group of retail customers first, and then try to find a serious distributor from among them. What's going to happen if you sell to people first is that they are going to think it is a selling business. If they don't think they can sell, then they're just not going to get anywhere. You might get them signed up to be a wholesale buyer, or they might sign up to get you off their back. But they're not going to be an active business builder.

There are three ways to build your business. Selling products first is the slowest. Sharing the business is faster. However, a lot of people are scared to death of the word "business." The fastest way is the Lifestyle approach. Ninety-five percent of the people want a better life—this means more time, money and good health.

In the process of doing this you're building a pipeline. You're moving the products. The slow way is to sell your products first and make the person think it is a selling business when it's not. In fact, it's really a teaching business. Using selling, they seem to think they've got to have some kind of experience with the products, no matter that a million people before them have used and enjoyed them. They've got to try them themselves to see if they work. Or they might think they're too expensive. Or all three. Selling first creates the wrong idea altogether.

People ask us, which do we prefer? The opportunity approach? Or the product approach? Actually, we don't really do either one, because there is an even faster way to build a business. The fastest way we've found is to use The System, which incorporates the Lifestyle approach.

CHAPTER 5

A Collection of Success:
Other Principles To Help You Succeed In Network Marketing

T his chapter contains discussion regarding several topics central to Network Marketing and how they can help you build your business. Of course, as you read, you can often apply the principles of The System to these topics, enhancing your understanding of The System even more. So read on, and find out some of the ways that Nancy and I have become so successful.

Residual Income

Sixteen years ago, we started in a company with four people. Today we have over 800,000 people in our downline. Last month, this organization grew by over 3,000 new members. Ninety-eight percent of all the new people came from the original four. Now, does that answer the question, "Do you need to sponsor a lot of people to build a large organization?" Obviously, you can see that you don't.

Notice I used the word "sponsor," not "recruit." I'll explain this in more detail later, but the point here is that this is a sponsor and teach business. How were we able to build such a large organization like this? We don't really work that hard, either. This is about working smart, not hard.

When you sponsor a new person into your organization, how long does it take you to teach that new person how to do the business? Can you do it in one or two hours? How about in two to three days? How about in two or three weeks? Do some of you have people you sponsored three to six months ago, and they still have not sponsored anybody yet?

Would you like to know why they haven't sponsored anyone yet? It's so simple when you think about it. The reason they have not sponsored anybody yet is because no one has shown them something that they think they can do.

The System is something that you can do—anybody you know can do—and once you see how The System works it will open up your mind about who you think you can talk to about your business. Once you realize that absolutely anyone can do this, you will no longer pre-judge anyone.

The great thing about The System is that it is very simple! Anybody can learn it in about 10 minutes or less (by reading Chapter 2 of this book or watching it on the DVD "The Napkin Presentations: Plus Using The System"). With these tools, a brand new person can learn enough information in ten minutes or less that they can actually start sponsoring. Not only will you be able to do this in ten minutes or less, but you're going to be able to do this without them having to know virtually anything about your company! That might have sounded impossible before you started reading this book, but hopefully after having read through The System you are saying to yourself, "Wow, I really don't have to know anything to get started!"

When I say "get started," I mean that a person has not started in this business until they have sponsored their first person. The quicker you can get your new person to sponsor someone, the better the chances are that person will stay around and make it.

Of the large organization we've built that I referred to earlier, over 90 percent live 6,000 to 7,000 miles away from our home in California. They live in Europe. They don't even read, speak or understand English. People constantly ask us how we did this.

The anwer is motivation. We don't really motivate them ourselves. What we do is teach the leaders self-motivators. Then the leaders teach it to their downlines.

What is a self-motivator? A self-motivator is something that when you are doing it, it's motivating yourself. So, all we did was teach the original four people the self-motivators. Then they taught their people, who then taught their people, etc. That way, everyone stays motivated continuously. It reinforces the idea every time you teach it.

Here is one of the self-motivators. (By the way, this works great at sizzle sessions, too.) You can practice teaching it to one another. It will give you a whole new look at what we call "residual income."

Most of you know what residual income is. It is money that keeps coming in long after you have done the work. Here is something to think about. Let's say that you are living in the home of your choice and you have no mortgage payments. In other words, you own the home—free and clear. You are driving the car of your choice. You have no car payment. You own the car. Your phone bills are current. Your credit cards are current. You have absolutely no bills at all. Now, if you were in that situation, and you were making $10,000 a month, every—month whether you get out of bed or not—you could live the lifestyle that is better than most millionaires.

Now, think about all your friends who are not in Network Marketing. How could they possibly have $10,000 a month coming in, whether they get out of bed or not, in the scenario I just described? Well, most of you have probably heard since you were young, "Wouldn't it be nice to have enough money in the bank so that you could live off the interest and never touch the principle?"

At today's current interest rates, the size of account you'd have to have in a bank where they'd actually send you a check each month for $10,000 interest would be a principle balance of approximately $6 million. How many people do you know who are going to be able to have $6 million in the bank by the time they retire? Could you have that much saved in the bank by the time you retire?

You see, I'm telling you that either you can save six million in order to receive $10,000 a month income, or you could be receiving $10,000 a month from your Networking company. Look at the difference. To get it from your Network company, you just sponsor four or five friends. And then you help them do the same, etc. By the time you get down four or five levels deep, you're going to have $10,000 a month coming to you.

What does a person have to do to put that kind of money in the bank, if they're not in Network Marketing? First, they need a job. From their job, they have to pay taxes on that income. They have to pay their mortgage payment, car payments, all their bills, braces on their children's teeth, etc. With the money they have leftover at the end of the week, they perhaps take the family out to a dinner. We call this "discretionary income." Then, beyond that, they might be saving up for their annual vacation (holiday). In America, that's one to two weeks. In Europe, that's four to six weeks.

After all this, whatever money they have left is what they are able to accumulate into a savings account towards the $6 million, or even the $3 million I mentioned before. The $3 million would give you the interest income of $5,000 a month.

So, what do you think is easier to do? To learn a system that you can teach a friend to do in ten minutes, so that they can go out and teach four or five friends how to do this business in ten minutes or less—or accumulate that much money in the bank?

Now, let me show you something else that I think you will find interesting. This will help you with your retention. Let's say that you have someone in your business who is making $200 a month. They've been working for about six months now. They say to you, "You know, this just doesn't seem to be going fast enough. I think I'm going to quit."

If they would just understand this presentation, they will never quit the business. And furthermore, remember "self-motivator," every time you show this to someone. It will remind you how important this is, and you will never quit the business either.

You see, it takes $100,000 in savings to provide a $200 a month interest income. Most people aren't making that much money in a year! Yet, in just six months working part-time in this business they're already making $200 a month.

We tell that person, "Well, rather than quitting, why don't you keep doing what you're doing, and by the end of the first year, you'll push that up to

$400 a month?" That would, by comparison, take $200,000 in bank savings.

In America last year, we had too many bankruptcies. The fact is, if 80% of those families who filed bankruptcy would have had between $200 to $400 extra coming in each month, they would not have been forced into it. You see, it is not always about making $5,000 to $10,000 a month. That is nice. But what about the hundreds upon hundreds of thousands of people who could simply use an extra $200 to $400 a month? What a difference that could make in their lives!

This presentation is easy to learn because we're just dividing in half. So, a $100 a month check would take $50,000 in the bank. $50 a month would take $25,000 in the bank. $25 per month would require $12,500 in savings. And $12.50/month would take $6,250 in the bank.

Now, why do I show figures so low? How many of you can remember your first check from Network Marketing? I just heard about a survey that recently revealed the average first commission check was about seven dollars. How then, you ask, can you get excited about that? How can you get excited about a check for a mere $12.50?

Well, once you really understand what this presentation represents, you really can get motivated. The person you sponsor today, that sponsors someone tomorrow, in their first month in this business ends making between $12.50 and $25.00. It's as if they just put $6,000 to $12,000 in the bank their first month in the business! How many of you can save the equivalent of $6,000 to $12,000 a month from your current jobs? Nobody is doing that.

So let's say you're just getting started. You need to build a solid foundation first. Please refer to Napkin Presentation #4, which teaches that you have to build a solid foundation before you can start putting up the building. At first, you don't see much income while you're getting started.

The first three to four months, you're growing at $12 to $25. Then from four to six months you're growing from $25 to $50. From six to eight months, you're growing at about $50 to $100. And from eight months up to one year, you're growing between $200 to $400 a month.

Now, understand that when you are growing between $100 and $400 a month it's just like you have put between $50,000 and $200,000 into a bank account. Have you ever thought that in your lifetime you could do that?

I believe that it is virtually impossible for almost anyone who has a job to be able to save $3 million in three years. However, I also believe that it is entirely possible for almost anyone who is willing to follow The System to build a residual income in that time frame that would pay them $5,000 a month. To put it another way, I'm saying that in three years you can put the equivalent of $3 million in the bank. The $5,000 spends the same. I don't know how you could do that—unless you are in Network Marketing!

When you understand the significance of this presentation, you get the feeling that you need to talk to everyone you know about this business. This presentation can be reviewed again and again until you completely understand it. It is also printed in the back of the book *The 45 Second Presentation That Will Change Your Life*. Once you see the power in it, you'll want everyone to know about it.

Your Best Prospects

People often ask us some of the reasons why we have been able to build such a large organization so fast. One of the main reasons is how we approach our business as compared to how most others approach building this business.

Our company has health products just as other companies do. But we don't see ourselves as selling health products because if we did we would only have 15 percent of the market to approach. That's because at any given time only about 15 percent of the population are sick, hurt or really into health. So we don't do that.

What we are doing is looking for people who would like to have a better life. That's why we wear the "Own Your Life" pin. It's a constant reminder that people want a better life. It's a balance. It's having both the time and the money to do whatever you want to do—when you want to do it.

We've traveled all over the free world for years. I would estimate that in all the countries we've traveled about 95 percent of the people we've met want to have a better life. It doesn't matter, either, where they are on the socioeconomic scale. You see, even if they have a $500,000 yacht, given an opportunity, the person would like to move up to a million dollar yacht. And then to a five million dollar yacht. There is always somewhere else to go.

What I'm saying is that 95 percent are looking for a better life. The other 5 percent already own their life. They already have the time and money they need. What we say about them is that they also want to live forever. They want to look good and feel good. So, they make great customers for our health products! With our attitude, we now have 100 percent of the people we can talk to because we don't talk to them about the products first.

People ask us all the time who the best prospects are for their business. I tell them, "You know what? It's really very simple. Your best prospect for your business is someone you already know who wants something." That is, something they can't get doing what they're doing now.

Do you know that a "couch potato" can be a prospect? They're sitting home watching that little 17-inch screen. Maybe they'd really like to have one of those 52-inch plasma flat screen sets? With The System, it's so simple to get started building a networking business, pretty soon they're able to get that big TV set. Then the Ferraris and all the toys on the big screen are looking more desirable. Maybe there's something else they want?

Here's a little story that really illustrates this point. Last year we were in Copenhagen, Denmark, driving up the coast to catch a ferryboat to Helsinborg, Sweden. This was on a Friday, a work day. As we were driving up there, looking out the window, we saw tens of thousands of sailboats in the marinas all along the coast. Once we were on the ferryboat, looking out over the water, guess what we didn't see? We did not see one sailboat. Not one. Why didn't we see any sailboats? Because they were all moored in the marinas. And why were they in the marinas? Because the people who own them were all at work.

Do you think they care about my products? Or my company? They could care less. I know that what they really care about is getting their sailboat out on the water. That's what they want to do. Right?

So all I have to do, using The System, is show them there's three steps in it. After they've seen the first two, they can see that they can build the business that will allow them to do this. Now they see they will need a "vehicle." So I show them the products, and they love them!

They don't have to try them for 30 days to see if they work. It has nothing to do with anything like that because they just want to get their sailboat out on the water. We have shown them how they can do it.

Now, think about other situations. For example, some people like to ski a lot. Wouldn't it be much better to be able to ski during the weekdays than on weekends when it's really crowded? Those are your prospects.

Think about how many people have little children at home. Here's what motivated us when we first got started. We have two sons, Doug and Greg. They wanted to be professional tennis players. We lived in the Northwest. It doesn't rain hard, but it rains a lot. You could go for six weeks without seeing the sun.

The boys couldn't get enough practice time indoors to become a professional at anything. So we moved our entire family to sunny Southern California where the sun shines almost all the time, and there are acres and acres of tennis courts.

They grew up in an era where they practiced two or three times a week with youngsters like Pete Sampress, Michael and Carl Chang, and they played in tournaments with Andre Agassi.

Let me tell you what all these kids, that made it in professional tennis, had in common. When they were little and getting started, they had to go to the tournaments so they could beat everybody in town. Then they went across town, across country, and across the world to compete in the circuit. What they all had in common was that their parents could be there with them.

Consider what sadly occurs at many Olympics. They were interviewing parents of the athletes on television in their homes—because they couldn't afford to be at the Olympics to watch their children participate.

When we first started following our boys around the tennis circuit, there were fewer than ten percent of the parents out there supporting their children. I will make you a guarantee. Ninety percent of the other parents had a lot more money than we did back then. But why weren't they out there? They did not have the time! Remember, all this is about a balance between time and money. We all know people who have a lot of money, but can they go watch their kids play soccer or football? We know there are a lot of retired people with plenty of time, but they don't have the money to go and visit their grandchildren whenever they want to. It doesn't matter what the sport is. It could be tennis, golf, ice-skating, etc. It could be anything.

The Napkin Presentations: *History in the Making*

Here's how all the Napkin Presentations were developed. The original book came out in May, 1981, and has since sold over four million copies and been translated into over 20 languages. For ten years before we had the book, we would sponsor someone using the product and vehicle approach. But before we would let the new person talk to their best friend, we would teach them what came to be known as the Napkin Presentations. It became known that way because we were usually in a coffee shop or restaurant and I'd just grab a napkin to draw diagrams and teach with.

Once the person knew the Napkin Presentations, they understood Network Marketing. We then coined the phrase, now they "know how to drive." We were very successful doing it this way. We continued doing it this way for ten years. It would take three or four hours with all the interruptions. Or if I was on long distance, the phone bill would be huge.

One day I finally said to Nancy, "Nancy, I'm really burned out from doing these long presentations. I just can't do this any more." So one Christmas holiday while we were in Phoenix and Tuscon, Arizona during our son's tennis tournaments, I made an outline of the Napkin Presentations.

When we got back to our home in the Northwest, with about 14 people in the room, we did our first audio taping of the Napkin Presentations. It was about an hour-and-a-half. Later on, in a studio, we condensed it to about one hour. My thinking at the time was, the next time I sponsor someone I can loan them the tape, and the tape can do the talking for me.

Probably one of the smartest (or luckiest) things I've ever done in my entire life (aside from marrying Nancy) was that I didn't mention the name of the company we were working with on the tape recording. And soon copies of this tape had made their way into the hands of distributors for several companies. Over the next few months tens of thousands of copies were sold.

From this tape we wrote the book The 45 Second Presentation That Will Change Your Life. *Since the first copies of the book came off of the press, I've never had to sit down with anyone and teach them anything that's in the book. I believe that everything in the book is very important for the new distributor to understand before they go and talk to their first prospect.*

This can be a real motivator. Let's say you have a youngster at home between four and eight years old just getting into a sport. You might be thinking that by the time the child is ready to really get out there, you want to have your act together with your business so that you can be out there with them.

We all have bad days, no matter what our profession. If you have a bad day, are you going to look at your child and quit when you remember that this was your goal? No. You're going to keep on working at it.

All About Salespersons

One of my favorite subjects is salespeople. Only five percent of the population are good salespeople. Ninety-five percent are non-salespeople. This is all about understanding. Most people don't understand this business. Most people don't understand the things I'm teaching you here because nobody ever explained it to them before.

Here's something that is very interesting. Most people join these Network Marketing companies—and there are a lot of them—but for some reason they end up looking for their prospects in this five percent pool of salespeople. Here is what happens when they do that. Let's say you sponsor a salesperson tomorrow. Within 30 to 60 days someone from another company comes along and tells your new person, "Hey, why don't you do this program, too?" Before you know it, your new person is trying to build a business in three or four different companies. We know that doesn't work.

We got rich teaching our people to work with the non-sales types—the 95 percent. When you think about this, it makes a lot of sense. There are more of them to talk to. There's no competition there, either, because everybody else is tripping over each other to get to the five percent. Now, here's what's really interesting. Why would you want to go out and look for someone for your business who has, historically in our industry, been the least successful of any group in this industry?

Think about that. Historically, salespeople have had the least chance of success in this industry. Now, if you happen to be a salesperson, you're in the right place. That's because salespeople can be a huge success in this business, but they must learn this business.

Here's what I mean. There are Network Marketing companies, and there are direct sales companies. They are different. They mix like oil and water. Most people don't know the difference. If you tell everybody in your downline right now, then should they happen to sponsor a salesperson they can pass it along, so they can understand the difference between sales and Network Marketing.

Buying Lunch: *A Fun Perspective*

Earlier in the book, when discussing how your sponsor is one of your best tools, I describe a typical scenario where you, your sponsor and your new prospect are all at lunch. Imagine you're all finished with the meal and the check is coming. The question is, who pays for the meal? Think about it. As the "senior" sponsor, I love this situation. Along with his prospect, my distributor invited me, the sponsor, to do the work (help describe the benefits of the "vehicle"). Therefore, he pays for the meal.

So here's the real question. How many times is he going to buy me a meal before he starts thinking, "I can do what Don just did. I don't need to keep buying his lunch. From here on, I'm going to try to go with someone in my downline. She can get a friend/prospect to come to lunch—and she'll pay for my meal."

Recently, we put on a seminar in Stuttgart, Germany. A fellow came up to me afterward and says, "Don, did you realize that if you do this business right, you would never have to buy a meal?" You know what? He's right.

It's very simple. A salesperson's whole life is about being recruited. Note the word "recruited." They have been recruited by a sales manager to sell for the sales manager. So when you recruit a salesperson into your company, here is what that person is thinking, "I'm going to go out and recruit a bunch of people to sell for me."

With that kind of thinking, they will never make it big in this business. We do not recruit people to sell for us. We sponsor people so that we can go to work for them. That is completely the opposite from what the salesperson is used to all their life. Here's an example of what I mean. I sponsor someone who then sponsors his or her friend. He or she goes to work for the friend. I also go to work for the friend. The friend then sponsors another friend. They both go to work for the new person, and I also go to work for that new person. We do this all the way down the line. The deeper you go, the stronger your business gets because everybody has people in their upline working for them.

I have seen salespeople come into this business and over a period of a few months literally recruit over a hundred people. The problem is, they are only one or two levels deep in a couple of places. They have not duplicated themselves one time. This is a business that is about duplication.

You are not duplicated in this business until the person you sponsor is three levels deep. So, if the frontline is me and I sponsor Kathy, I am not duplicated until Kathy is three levels deep. Kathy and I must help three new people in her downline. Most salespeople never learn to duplicate. Please see Napkin Presentation #4, which explains this procedure in detail.

What salespeople do, because they don't understand, is sign up ten people their first month. You get excited because it looks like they're on fire and you're going to be rich. The second month they go out and sign up ten more. The third month they go get ten more. By now they're losing their first ten from the first month. By the time they get to the sixth month, they're off looking for the next hot deal to sell.

They will make more money than we will doing it our way during the first six months. But we will go by them like they are standing still between six to nine months! That's because, when you do it our way, you play the game we call "duplication." The salesperson was playing a game called "adding and subtracting."

The biggest asset a salesperson has is the ability to call on and meet strangers. It is that strength that also becomes their reason for failure because all they're doing is running around signing people up. They don't spend enough quality time with any one person to get the duplication process going.

On the other hand, for the non-sales types, it is uncomfortable to call on strangers. So the non-sales type will sponsor a few friends. Then they will help them with their friends. And then help them with their friends, and on and on. It starts out slower, but it gains momentum.

We know it is uncomfortable for non-sales people to talk to strangers. Here is one sentence that can drive your whole business. Anyone can meet a stranger—but only if someone will introduce the stranger to them. I will explain this statement in detail later in this book.

If you understand the context of that statement, you can break it down into two simple sentences for what a person needs to do to be successful. Make a friend. Meet their friends. You can actually practice this when you go to bed at night. Instead of counting sheep to go to sleep, just keep repeating to yourself, "I'm going to make a friend. And then meet their friends." Just keep saying it until you fall asleep. Guess what happens the next day?

Acres of Diamonds, Fields of Gold

Many years ago, a man who lived in Africa sold his farm because he wanted to go looking for diamonds. He traveled all over the African continent searching for the precious stones. Sadly, he had little luck in his search. Finally, after years of struggle, disappointment, and desperation, he ended his miserable life by drowning himself in the ocean.

Ironically, the person to whom this man sold his farm eventually discovered the Kimberly mine on that very farm. That's right—the largest diamond mine in Africa was located on the very plot of land sold by the original farmer, who foolishly left it in order to go looking for diamonds elsewhere!

Here's another story, which took place during the great gold rush era in California. A man named Sutter, who hailed from Switzerland, bought a farm in the foothills near Sacramento. Who did he buy it from? That's right—a man who went off to look for gold in other parts of the state. As you've probably guessed (or already knew), Mr. Sutter discovered the largest gold field in the state on the same land tract sold by the fellow who went looking elsewhere for riches!

My point is this: I want you to recognize your acre of diamonds and your field of gold. Teach the people you already have in your group how to talk to the people they already know so that when it is appropriate, they can introduce them to you. In the process of meeting the friends of your friends, in coffee shops or restaurants, you will eventually become involved with more people than you will ever know what to do with.

Our Thoughts On Time

How often have you had someone tell you that they don't have time to do this business? Time is the number one excuse that people have for not doing this business.

The most important thing you can learn about this business is this: how you approach a friend and talk about this business is how they think this business is. In other words, if you go to someone's home and do a party plan or an in-home presentation, and you are there for two or three hours, they could absolutely love your vehicle (products, company, etc). But guess what? They are going to say, "You know, this is really great, but I don't really have time to do this."

They now think that in order to do this business, they're going to have to spend two or three hours a night in people's homes, planning and arranging parties, just to build a business. For many, it seems like too much hassle, cost and time, and it turns them away.

Here's another example. Let's say you pick someone up at 7 pm to take them to an opportunity meeting. After the meeting you stop at the coffee shop. You get them home about 10 pm. They say to you, "You know, I really had a great time. But I really don't want to do this."

If they had such a good time, why don't they want to do the business? It's simple—they think that what the business is about is picking people up and spending all this time at meetings, going out for coffee, etc. They don't have the time to do all that.

Here are some things that will help you. If you are going to take a prospect to a meeting, be sure to tell them at least three times before you get there that this is only one of several ways to do our business. If you don't tell them that, they will think that going to meetings is the only way they can do it. Maybe they don't want to go to a meeting every Tuesday night because it's their favorite TV night, or their children have a soccer match, or something. Or perhaps they just moved here from another area and they wouldn't know who they could get to go to a meeting anyway.

Preferably, you don't have any more opportunity meetings. You convert them to weekly training meetings. They are so much more effective. It's okay to bring a guest to a training meeting. You tell your friend that you are having a "special" training meeting. They are always "special," and held on Tuesday evening. It's where we teach our people how to do the business.

Now here's the difference. Let's say you have an opportunity meeting with 40 people in the room. You would probably be very lucky if eight of them were actually guests. Usually someone is up in front of the room in a suit or something, looking like a salesperson, talking to the guests. The guests have their arms crossed, which is the body language for non-committed, because they know that person at the front of the room is going to try to sell them something.

Meanwhile, all the members, especially the ones whose guests didn't show up, are counting the spots in the ceiling because they are bored to death. They have already heard this presentation twenty times. Here is something really amazing. There are actually opportunity meetings like this being held—and there aren't even any prospects there! What is that all about? Everybody there is already in the business.

So, I say let's not do those any more. Let's just do training meetings. They're not boring because you can have training A, B, C and D. Training A could be about your vehicle (company, product, marketing plan). Training B could be about what you are learning in this book. Training C could be about the Napkin Presentations. You can get together with the leaders and decide what you're going to have at these training meetings. This is so that when a new person gets started, they know that once they have attended trainings A through D they have completed all their training.

With this type of meeting, the person conducting the meeting is no longer talking to the guests. It's a training meeting. So now, instead of being uneasy about someone trying to sell them something, the guests are very relaxed. The guests are privileged to be listening in on the training.

Remember, it takes only ten minutes to teach The System. You always budget ten minutes to teach The System whether you have one guest or ten guests. They will all sign up. Here's why. They came to the meeting because they were looking for something. When you show them that it only takes ten minutes to teach a new person this business, you just showed them something they can do—they're not going to be intimidated by this new opportunity. You don't have to know anything to get started in this business. We rarely ever miss a guest who comes to a training meeting and learns how easy this is with The System. You get as close to 100 percent sign-ups as you possibly can get. Plus, the meetings are a lot more fun this way. Give it a try. You will be amazed how well this will work for you.

Working Hard vs. Working Smart

Next, I want to share with you the difference between working hard and working smart.

Working Hard

First, I'll discuss working hard. Let's say I've just sponsored a person into the business after using the first two steps. If they come into the business, I let them keep the book. If they don't sign up, I get the book back.

My new prospect does the first two steps, and then loans the book to his friend. Next he goes to another friend, and he repeats the first step ("The 45 Second Presentation" part), but now he is not able to do the second step. Then he goes to his next friend and does the first step. But, again, he can't do the second step.

He keeps repeating this process. Why can't he do the second step? Because he only had one copy of the book. The very first person still has the book. She went on a two-week vacation, and didn't take the book along. She comes back from the vacation. She reads the book. Then she starts thinking, "You know, all he did was ask me if I knew anybody who likes to travel or go on vacation (holiday). Then he told me about the three things it takes—money, time and health. And he loaned me this book. I can do that."

She then decides to come into the business. So she keeps the book. Meanwhile, all this time has gone by with several people still waiting to read this book that they weren't going to get anyway. That is what we call "working hard," or working the "hard" way.

Working Smart

Working smart means having enough books (tools) on hand so that when you do Step One, you can do Step Two right away. Here is a final review. You can actually practice this two-step process at home at night before you go to bed.

Stand in front of a full-length mirror. In one hand, you have your lifestyle business card with the "The 45 Second Presentation" on it, which is Step One (we call it "this"). In your other hand, you have a copy of the book, *The 45 Second Presentation That Will Change Your Life*, which is Step Two (we call it "that"). Now practice—do "this," do "that." Do "this," and do "that." Isn't that easy?

If you can ask a couple of questions, explain the three things it takes to travel, and find someone to teach how to do "this" and do "that," then you can absolutely be successful in this business.

Biggest "Waste-of-Time Things" People Do To Build Their Business

We have a list we call "waste-of-time things to do" in building your business. The second thing on the list is explaining a marketing plan in detail to a new person. Don't do it. By the time you get all the way through it, they don't understand it anyway. Just give them enough to get started. It's not necessary to explain the whole thing. Keep it real simple.

Also, the companies have evolved with the tools, things like the computer, the brochures, and the websites. Speaking of computers, the computer almost caused the downfall of this industry for a few years. People thought that all they had to do was recruit using computers. Well, it doesn't work. Computers are only good for sift and sorting as explained in Step 1 of The System, training, follow-up and communication. It does not work to blast cyberspace to recruit people.

The point here is, once you have all the tools, all you have to do with the prospect is direct them to the right tools and then follow up if she (he) has any questions.

Tragically, the number one waste-of-time thing that people do in trying to build their business is to look for people to sponsor into their business. If you do the business right, you will never have to do that.

Instead, you start off with a friend. A lot of people, however, say that they are willing to talk to strangers, but don't want to talk to their friends. Their problem is one of two things. Either they don't believe it, or they don't understand it.

If you believe that you could be financially independent in 1 to 3 years, and you understand it well enough to explain it to them (or at least loan them the book to explain it for you) why would you want to give that kind of an opportunity to a total stranger before you gave it to your best friend?

Of course, you start with your friend. That person will know about 200 people that you don't know. You teach the one you already have (your friend) how to do "this" and "that," and how to introduce you to their friends. Remember when I said earlier that anyone can meet a stranger if someone will introduce the stranger to them?

It is only appropriate, however, after they have read the book. If he gets me on the phone with the prospect, the first thing I will say is, "Have you read the book?" If she says, "Uh, no. I just got it today and I plan to read it tonight," I tell her, "Great. Why don't we continue this conversation tomorrow—after you've read the book." You don't want to talk to someone until after they've read the book. Otherwise, you'll get all those same questions I answered for ten years before becoming burned out. So it's only appropriate to talk after they've read the book.

The Power Of One

I want to stress something here. After I have signed up one of my friends, I immediately help them turn around and get their first person. Do the same with your new distributors. Then start working downline to get the duplication going. In the process of doing this, along comes a second person. Now I have two people that I'm working with.

This business has never been about signing up a bunch of people. It's about this—you get one person, and then help that person get one person. Then you teach and help that person to sign up one more. Meanwhile, you start over and get one more. Then you have a real flow going.

Once you get up to five—if you are working for your people like you should be—you now are going to be really busy. Remember that each person knows over 200 others. Some people misunderstand this. They say that we tell them you only sponsor five people. That's not true. Once you get the five, you put the brakes on for a moment and work with them until one of the five doesn't need you any more. It could be the first person you brought in. It might be the last one. It doesn't matter. When that person no longer needs you, you're free to offer someone else the opportunity.

When you stop to think about it, isn't that what's really great about this business? You get to choose the people you want to have this great opportunity.

You should have up to five new people by the end of your first full month in the business. If you start somewhere in the middle of a month, then you start counting after the first month in the business.

Before I continue, I'm going to tell you about a huge mistake that is commonly made in this business. This is a mistake you want to avoid. Like I mentioned earlier, most of your prospects will know about 200 people with whom they could share their newfound opportunity. However, never, ever tell your new person to make out a list of 100 or 200 names. Don't do it—and here's why.

You've done all this preliminary work of telling someone that this business is not selling, it's networking and Network Marketing is different than selling. The person finally signs up in your business. This person might have had a job 15 years ago selling vacuum cleaners, insurance, encyclopedias or whatever. Guess what the first thing a sales manager tells the salesperson to do? Make a list of 100 names. Can anyone explain to me why you would need a list of 100 names simply to sponsor your best friend? You know who your best friends are.

Instead, compile a short list. What's a short list? If you were to look up our website, you would see that we have cruise dates posted all the time. Everyone is welcome to come along on our cruises. If you were to go on one of those cruises, think of the five people who you would like to see have the time and money to be able to come with you. That is your list of names!

By the time you start meeting their friends, and meeting their friends, and so on, you're going to be so busy that you just have no idea how it grows. I showed you how we started with just four people. We spend a month in Europe. All we do while we're there is go around and meet people. That's all we do. So don't tell anyone to make out those big lists, or they'll think this is about selling.

If we take a look at the figures, we see that 5 multiplied by 200 is 1,000. You now have a thousand potential people to meet through the five you already have. Just teach the ones you already have, how to do "this" and "that" so they can introduce new people to you.

You're going to help your 5 people so they get 5 serious people. That takes you to 25 serious people. You should be there by the end of 3 full months in the business—25 multiplied by 200 equals 5,000. These 5,000 plus the original 1,000 adds up to 6,000 potential people to meet through the people you already have. When would you have time to be out looking for strangers?

You're going to teach your people to help their people. It now goes from 25 up to 125. That's 25 multiplied by 5 each. You should be there in about six months. But, if it takes a whole year, so what? These are all serious people here. Now, you have 125 multiplied by 200, which equals 25,000. Now your potential number of people to meet has reached 31,000 through the people you already have. When would you have time to be looking for strangers?

Making A Friend

As I've explained in the book, probably the easiest way to be successful in Network Marketing is to make a friend, then meet their friends. The following story helps illustrate why this principle is true.

Many years ago we were having dinner in a Chart House restaurant in San Diego with our sons Douglas and Greg. While there, we learned of a promotion where if you ate in all 65 Chart House restaurants, you would get around-the-globe airfare for two. We knew that night when we signed up that we were going to accomplish this.

Back then (1995) there were twenty Chart Houses scattered all over California. I remember going to Florida for ten days to eat in nine Chart House restaurants. There were four in the Caribbean and four in Hawaii. One was located in Vancouver, Washington and one in Vancouver, Canada.

Several were located near Denver and another in New Orleans. There were a bunch from Washington, D.C. to Boston, Massachusetts.

Well, after a year and a half, we did it. We ate in every Chart House existing at that time. Though there were over 320,000 people who registered, we were among the mere thirty-two people that actually accomplished it.

When we were in Massachusetts, eating at our next to last Chart House, the entire restaurant staff had a greeting line for us and a special insert in the menu saying, "Congratulations Don & Nancy Failla—only one to go!" Needless to say we had a good time doing this and we met many very nice people. Yet here's the important part of the story.

Because we had both registered for the promotion, we each received two tickets to fly around the world. Our first flight we went to Hawaii for two weeks, then to Hong Kong for one week, Bangkok for one week, Istanbul for a week, one week in Athens, a week in London, and finally home to California.

When we were in Istanbul, Turkey, we stayed at the Conrad Hilton. In the morning we were heading out for the day and walking down the street. Coming toward us were two men, each of them wearing large buttons that were in English. When they were next to us I stuck out my hand and said, "Hi. I am Don Failla." One of them said, "You're Don Failla? I just faxed your office yesterday because I would like to translate your book into Turkish."

This was like winning the lottery. There are over 70 million people in Turkey and we run into probably the only one person in the country that had my book, and he had a German translation of it.

The next day Thomas came into town and gave us a great tour of Istanbul. The next day his wife, Elif, who is Turkish, came in and gave us a great tour of the grand bazaar and shopping. Thomas stayed home because if he had come then Elif would not speak English. She would rely on him to speak. However, the next day they both came and we all had a fantastic time. We had dinner together at the Orient House. We were making friends.

Several months later we took a second trip around the world. We went to the United Kingdom first, then on to Sweden. From there we ended up in Frankfurt, Germany, where Thomas had organized a seminar for us. After the seminar, we were going to go back to Turkey for ten days.

There is a moral to this story. Thomas and Elif joined us in our networking business. Today, we have over 100,000 members in our downline from their efforts. Do you see? All we did was "make a friend" and then "meet their friends."

CHAPTER 6
How To Use The Own Your Life Pin And Other 45 Second Tools

Nancy and I wear the Own Your Life pin everywhere we go. When people ask us about the pin we tell them that "Owning Your Life" is having the time and money to do what you want to do, when you want to do it. This also allows us to start a conversation and ask the person a question—"Do you know anyone that likes to travel and go on holiday?" Now I am right into the first step of the system. The pin gives us an opportunity to get started talking to our prospect about lifestyle first. If we wore a pin that has our company name on it and they ask what it is then we end up starting with step three first: talking about our company and products. As soon as you mention a product to them they think you are trying to sell them something.

You should get everyone in your organization wearing the pin. This will benefit your whole organization. Let me give you an example. Nancy and I go on a lot of cruises. If we are by ourselves on a cruise and there are 3,000 other passengers we might get a few people during the course of the week that will ask us about the pin. But when we are having an "un-convention" cruise and we have thirty or forty people with us and they are all wearing the pin then everyone gets 50 to 60 people asking about it. With 40 people wearing the pin and moving around the other 3,000 passengers see the pin everywhere. Their curiosity about the pin goes up so high that they want to know what it means.

What I just described about wearing the pin on a cruise will also work in your own area. If you are the only one wearing it you will get people from time to time asking you about it. If you get everyone in your group wearing it all the time, this will increase the curiosity in your community and your whole organization will benefit.

People ask us what the pin is made of and we say solid gold. Then we tell them that we are just kidding but the pin is worth more than solid gold.

If one person asks you about it and you get into the right conversation with them and they come into your business then that can be worth way more than solid gold.

People all over the world wear the pin. It is very popular in Japan and Germany even though the pin is in English. When someone in Japan is wearing a pin in English it just raises the curiosity. In Denmark they wear the pin upside down. Nancy said to them, "Why are you wearing the pin upside down?" The answer was that when people see it they want to straighten it and then they ask about it. It is a perfect segue into The System.

When Nancy is shopping or in the grocery store and she notices someone looking at the pin but they are too shy to ask about it, she simply says to them, "I bet you want to know what that means." She can then hand them her card with The 45 Second Presentation on it. It is a great way to make new contacts and friends. Remember the first thing you have to do with someone you meet is to make a connection with them. You need to make a friend. The pin is a great door opener.

With the right tools this business can be a lot of fun and can grow very fast.

DON'T try to explain the entire marketing plan on a street corner or when your prospect is supposed to be working,

Distributors ask, "At what point do I show the new person the Napkin Presentations?" The answer is simple, "I don't." I give them a book or the Audio Book and I set a time in the near future when I can get back with them and discuss the material. After they have read the book or listened to the CD, there isn't that much to discuss. Now it's time to sponsor them and get to work helping them to sponsor someone else.

By giving your prospect *The 45 Second Presentation* book and "The Own Your Life" CD, that gets them through the material twice. The second time through they will get more out of it. If you just give them the book, it's unlikely that they will read it twice, or in the case of giving them the CD only, that they would listen to it twice. Also consider the fact that you don't know whether the person gets more from listening or reading. If they do both, it's almost guaranteed they will take in enough information to convince them that Network Marketing is something that even they can do successfully.

I suggest that you purchase ten sets of *The 45 Second Presentation* book and the CDs to supply your down-line. The sooner you put these tools to work for you, the sooner your organization will grow. Again, TEACH your people the steps to success. These books and CDs will teach them the fundamentals. Then, you can follow up by sharing your personal success experiences.

You can have the most fantastic "vehicle" in the industry, but until your distributors or representatives know how to "drive," they are simply not going to get anywhere.

When you teach distributors or representatives the presentations in this book, you are teaching them truly how to "drive." Bringing a new person on your "vehicle" without teaching them to "drive" is a waste of time—yours and theirs!

The 45 Second Presentation that Will Change Your Life should be used as a give-away for your new distributors. When they are ready to learn more, they can purchase the 45 Second Toolbox that contains all of the Failla training tools.

CHAPTER 7

More On Using "The System" With Your Cold Market

What is the difference between your cold market and warm market? Your warm market is your friends, or in other words people you know. The better the friend the warmer he or she is. Your cold market is people you do not know. They are the people you meet in line at the grocery store or the people you meet at the gas station. We teach that if you do the business right and sponsor a friend, then meet his or her friends, etc., then you should never run out of people to talk to about your business. But what about the people who get into your business who have already been in so many networking companies or other business ventures that when their friends see them coming they run the other way? These people are members of what is known as the NFL club. No Friends Left. So, how are they going to build a business?

As a brief recap, working in the cold market there are several tools you are going to need. You should always wear your Own Your Life pin. You never know when someone is going to ask you about it. You should also have the personalized Lifestyle Business Cards or Pass-Out Cards and you should have the IOwnMyLife.net prospecting site. Let me tell you once more how all these tools can work together to develop your cold market.

By wearing your Own Your Life pin everywhere you go, someone is bound to ask you what your pin means. You say, "It is about having the time and money to do what you want, whenever you want." Then you follow up with, "But let me ask you a question. Do you know anyone that likes to travel and go on vacation/holiday?" If they say no, you are finished because why would you want to try and sponsor someone that does not know any-one that likes to have fun? Remember, you get to choose the people you go to work for. Now imagine that they say that they do like to travel, or they may even say, "Yeah, I like to have fun." Now it is your turn again to follow up with, "You know, it takes three things to travel and go on vacation/holiday. It takes Time, Money and your Health. If I can show you how you could have all three would you be interested?"

It is either yes or no. If they say no, you are finished. Isn't it exciting to know this after just about a minute than to get a no after you have done two- or three-hour presentation?

Most people will say yes, so now you hand them your personalized Lifestyle Business Card and tell them to read the back of the card and check out your web site when they get home, which is of course your prospecting website that doesn't mention your company specifically (Step 1 of the System).

It is important here that you do not hand them a card that has your company name or product on it. If you do, they will ask you about it and now you skip step two and have moved on to step three of The System and you still don't even know if they want to take the time to learn how to drive. Remember, we do not want to show them or talk about the vehicle (company, product and marketing plan) until they know how to drive. They will know how to drive once they have read the book *The 45 Second Presentation That Will Change Your Life*. Once they do read it they will understand Network Marketing and then we say, "They know how to drive."

Somewhere between the time you give them your personalized OWN YOUR LIFE business card and when they get home, they will read the back of your business card which has the 45 Second Presentation (not to be confused with the book) written on the back. Simply tell them to read the back of the card and when they get home and to check out your website. When they do this they will know a little bit about you because you have your own personal story on your web site.

IOwnMyLife.net Tip

Make sure that when you are personalizing your site with your story that you do not mention your vehicle. This is a common mistake. They are not ready for Step 3 until they get through Step 2 (Step 2, you will remember, is reading The 45 Second Presentation *book.*

On your IOwnMyLife.net site, your prospects will see the advantages of owning a home-based business via the articles and videos that you can post on your site from our library of media. Prospects who are interested, are encouraged to fill out the survey questionnaire with their personal contact details. This information is delivered to you in an email as well as posted in your back office for future reference. As an added bonus when prospects submit their questionnaire, the site will send them Step 2 of the system right away (the first 4 chapters of *The 45 Second Presentation That Will Change Your Life* book).

Once a prospect has filled out the questionnaire and you now know more about their ambitions and past, you are on the path of converting that person from your cold market to your warm market. That is the whole purpose of the site. That person trusted you enough to provide you information that gives you insight into this person's life. You now can call him or her without the pressure of having to explain that the opportunity you have to offer is a home-based business—the site does that for you. Now it is up to you to make a connection with the person.

You know about them because they filled out the questionnaire. Now what do you do?

You give them a call and the most important thing is to make a connection with this person. You make a friend and you do this by small talk. When you are ready for your presentation, it should go like this:

I would like to ask you a few questions so I will know and you will know if this is something that you could do. First question: Do you think you could ask your friends if they know anyone that likes to travel and go on vacation/holiday? If the answer is no then you are finished trying to sponsor them. Why would you want to sponsor someone who does not know anyone that likes to have fun?

They, for the most, part will say, "Yes." This is your first yes.

Second question: Do you think you could tell them that it takes three things to travel and go on vacation/holiday? Those three things are time, money and your health. They say, "Yes." This is your second yes.

Third question: Could you ask your friend, "If I can show you how you could have all three things, would you be interested?" They say, "Yes," and now they have said YES three times.

Now you simply say, "I sent you the firt 4 chapters in email of a book, I would like to send you the full book so you can understand our industry. Give me your street mailing address and I will send it right out and after a few days we can talk again." It is a good idea to send the book Priority Mail. Most people are not used to getting mail this way and it conveys a sense of importance.

If they press you for what company, simply tell them that anyone can be successful if they follow The System, and if you start talking about the company, products, and marketing plan at this point you would not be following The System. If someone really wants something and they understand our industry (this also means they know how to drive), they will get on anything you show them. This is why The System works for all networking companies.

You should be aware that if you are talking to someone who has already been in network marketing and they press you for the Vehicle, it is okay to tell them; however, let them know that we want people to follow The System if they want to build their business successfully and in the fastest way possible.

When a person reads the book there is no guarantee that he or she is going to do your business. What is guaranteed is that you don't have to spend three hours of your time explaining Network Marketing to them.

You can see why you need the prospecting web site. The web site acts as a bridge between meeting someone and loaning them the book. The System will not work if you go to the mall and stop people. If you did stop someone in the mall and loan them the book on the spot, you are not really loaning the book; you are giving it away because you will never see it again.

When you are working with your warm market, you loan the book and since it is a friend you can get it back if your friend doesn't come into the business. If they come in, we always let them keep it. When you approach strangers and give them a book, like I said, you will never see it again. You could easily give away 100 books a day with zero results. The important thing to know is for The System to work you have to make a friend first.

Now you understand why you need the prospecting web site for that bridge between meeting a stranger, making a friend, and then loaning them the book.

Another Approach To Cold Market

We fly a lot and there is plenty of time to get to know one or more of the flight attendants, especially on international flights. We know they are all concerned about layoffs and most of them have lost their retirement. When we are getting off the plane we say to them,"You should check out what we do. Read the back of this card and when you get home check out our web site." In a few days we get an email with all the answers to the questions from our survey online and then we call them, make a friend and send a book. After a few days we get back to them or simply email them our company web site and tell them to check it out and get back to us if they have any questions. We have signed up many people over the years doing it exactly this way.

Let me give you an idea about using The System along with running a real simple ad. Many years ago we ran an ad on Fridays for three months in the *U.S.A. Today* newspaper and the ad said, "JOIN DON AND NAN-CY FAILLA'S WINNING TEAM AND BECOME A LIFESTYLE TRAINER. 1 800 XXX XXXX." We received several hundred calls from this ad. The number one question everyone had was, "How much will I get paid?" We then had to explain to them that this was their own business and was not a job. This was less effective, not to mention a lot of work on our part.

A few years ago we ran the same ad and instead of our 800 number, we put in our prospecting web site. We only received about 50 responses, but these were all people who had access to a computer and already knew it was a home-based business before we even talked to them. If you want to try this I would recommend that you change the ad to the following: JOIN (Your Name)'S FUN TEAM AND BECOME A LIFE-STYLE TRAINER (YOUR WEB SITE). The web site we have now from Sound Concepts is ten times better than the one we have been using for the last several years. You can see the new ones by going to www.IOwnMyLife.net or www.45SecondTools.com.

Other Ways of Using THE SYSTEM in the Cold Market

Nancy and I love to go on cruises. We have been on 56 weeks' worth of cruises and have a bunch more scheduled. Every year we have our un-convention cruise, on which you are all welcome to join us. There are networkers from all over the world and all different companies that join us on the un-convention cruise. We purposely choose the newest, biggest ships to go on. By choosing these ships there are, not including the group of networkers that join us, at least 3,000 prospects, I mean passengers.

If Nancy and I were the only two people on the cruise wearing the Own Your Life Pin we may get 5 to ten people that will ask us about it and then we can transition right into The System. Now let's say it is an un-convention cruise and we have 40 couples with us and everyone has a pin and wears it all the time. Since the 3,000 people are moving around and our 80 are moving around, you cannot go five to ten minutes without seeing one of these pins. The curiosity level goes up so high that by the end of the week, every one of the 40 couples has had 50 to 60 people ask them about the pin. Do you realize that it only takes one person who you meet this way to get into your business and get serious to pay for your cruise? What they do in six months to one year could more than pay for your cruise.

What I just described above works in your local area. If you are the only one wearing the pin, you will get people asking you about it from time to time. However, if your whole team wears them, it creates more curiosity. Can you imagine going into a restaurant with 15 to 20 people all wearing the pin? You will be amazed at what can happen.

Now what is an un-convention? Many years ago we got thinking about conventions and realized that they are usually held in beautiful resorts and people do not have time to enjoy the facilities because they are in meetings all the time. The problem was that they really learned the most at the breaks sharing ideas with other successful distributors. So we said let's have un-conventions and have no meetings. It is just one big break. We did this for thirteen years in Las Vegas and then we discovered that doing these on cruise ships was even more fun. Remember, as Nancy says, "The more fun you have the faster your business will grow." So we have no meetings; however, we do have a lot of Sizzle Sessions. You can read about Sizzle Sessions in *The 45 Second Presentation* book. It is napkin presentation number eight.

If you would like to join us on our next un-convention cruise, you can! Look for our next sailing on Sound Concepts' web site at www.45secondtools. com, then click on "Events." We would love to have you with us; the more people who come with us, the more pins that are walking around the cruise ship. The more pins walking around the more people will ask everyone who is wearing a pin about it. Plus the Sizzle Sessions are a perfect time to see what others are doing that you may be able to incorporate into your business.

More Ideas for the Cold Market

When you are in line at the grocery store, nine times out of ten there is a person in front of you or behind you with a huge basket full of groceries. They may make a comment about how everything is so expensive. What a perfect setup. All you have to say to them is, "You should be doing what we are doing." They say, "What's that?" and then you hand them your Lifestyle Business Card and tell them read the back and check out your web site.

We drive a Hummer II and lots of times at the gas station people comment about the price of gas. We just say that we are not concerned about it and that they should be doing what we are doing. Hand them the card and tell them to check out the web site.

We also recommend doing what is called the third-party approach. This is where you ask someone if they know anyone who would like some extra income, a better life, or whatever. Usually they will say, "I do." At this point, give them your Lifestyle Business Card or Pass-Out Card and have them read the 45-second presentation and tell them to check out your web site when they get home.

Here is a simple idea that has no rejection. When you pay your bills put in your Lifestyle Business Card. Someone has to open the envelope and they are doing this all day long and are bored to death. They look at your card and read The 45 Second Presentation and when they get home they can check out your prospecting web site. They could very well fill out the questionnaire. When you get the questionnaire you give them a call and make a friend and decide if you want to invest in sending them a book.

At your Sizzle Sessions you can get really creative on ways to get you card out. You never know when someone is going to respond. The System makes all this possible since you do not have to talk. One of the secrets to The System is to *not* talk. The more you talk the more the prospects think they don't have time and the more you talk the more they think they can *not* do what you are doing.

Buying email addresses and prospecting with the computer is not recommended. I do not know one person who has ever made this work. The problem is, no connection is made with the people you contact, and if they do sign up they never last, they are on to the next hot deal that comes along. There have been so many people who have tried this that most people, when they get an email from someone they don't know, just delete it. Do not waste your time and money on this. The computer is fantastic for follow-up communication and training once you have made a connection.

Buying leads is not for everyone; however, I do know a few people who have made it work. It usually takes a strong sales type and someone who can handle lots of rejection. In most cases the leads you buy have been sold to several people so now you have competition. I still say if you make a friend and meet their friends, you will never run out of people to talk to about your business.

When you are at a party or social event and you meet some new people, during the course of your conversation you can ask them what they do. When you ask people what they do, nine out of ten will tell you and then ask you what you do. Just tell them that you are a lifestyle trainer and you teach people how to have a better life. Then hand them your Lifestyle Business Card and tell them when they have a minute to read the back of the card and check out your web site. This is something that anyone can do. Anyone can hand someone they meet an Lifestyle Business Card and ask him to check out the web site. Not everyone will check out your web site, but remember that you really don't need everyone. Just one will be fine.

Conclusion

The thing that is exciting about The System, both in your warm market and cold market, is that you do not have to learn to say much because the tools take over and do all the talking for you. When you realize that you can teach someone to do this business in less then ten minutes with out them knowing anything, you suddenly realize that you have a lot of people to talk to.

CHAPTER 8
The Gallery Of Gems:
Key Ideas And Fun Phrases By Don & Nancy Failla

T he following are some of our favorite phrases (a few are just fun, most have a nugget of wisdom), as well as some of the core ideas we've incorporated into our successful business. And here's a suggestion. Gather some friends around in a Sizzle Session, and read and discuss these statements. It can stimulate a lot of fun thoughts and ideas of your own.

Don's Favorites

• If you want your dreams to come true, then wake up.

• Make a friend, meet their friends.

• Teach your people how to do "this," and then do "that."

• Anyone who thinks Networking has anything to do with sales will never make it big in this business, with very few exceptions.

• The computer is a great asset to building your business so at least learn to do emails.

• Non-sales types think selling is talking someone into something they do not need or want.

• This is a sponsor and teach business, not a recruit and sell business.

• Network Marketing is building a family of consumers.

• You don't recruit people to sell for you, sponsor people so you can go to work for them.

• You are not duplicating unless the person you sponsor is three levels deep.

• The secret to The System is not to talk; let the tools do the talking.

• The more you talk, the more your prospect thinks they don't have time, then they think they cannot do what you're doing.

- Salesmen can be huge in this business, provided they are willing to learn this business.
- The number one excuse people have for not doing the business is time.
- Anyone can meet a stranger if someone will introduce the stranger to them.
- Watch out for eavesdroppers.
- If you can't talk to your friends about your Networking business, then you either don't believe it or don't understand it.
- When one understands this business, we then say they know how to drive.
- If you want to see a pyramid, go to Egypt.
- To duplicate down more than two levels you need a simple System.
- You can teach your friend The System in less than ten minutes.
- Eliminate the word "sell" from your vocabulary.
- Five percent of any population are the good sales types; 95 percent are the non-sales types. Learn to build with the non-sales types—there's no competition and there are more of them to talk to.
- Teach your prospects how to drive before you show them your vehicle.
- Would you let your best friend go for a drive around the block in your brand new hot sports car if they did not know how to drive?
- You can work hard in the beginning for almost nothing and hardly work at all in the future and make a fortune.
- Making one new friend can make a difference.
- The more you know, the slower you grow.
- Only take advice from people who are currently building a business.
- A hundred-name list is sales talk, not Network Marketing.
- A short list is okay.
- Teach the people you already have how to talk to people they already know.

- If you're doing the business right, you never have to look for strangers.
- Your acre of diamonds is the people you already know.
- A sizzle session is about getting together to share ideas.
- When you have a job you are helping someone else reach their dreams.
- Find someone who wants something then show them how The System can help them get it.
- Two things happen when you talk too much to your prospect. They think they don't have time and they think they cannot do what you're doing.
- The Own Your Life movement is on around the world.
- The Own Your Life pin is not made from solid gold; however, it is worth much more.
- Without a map you could get lost.
- Real men don't ask directions.
- It is hard to teach salespeople not to talk.
- This business is about multiplication, not addition and subtraction.
- What do you want?
- Sell your products or service to a non-sales type first, and they will always think this is a selling business.
- Network Marketing and sales mix like oil and water: they don't.
- There are Network Marketing companies, and there are direct sales companies and they're different.
- Let the tools do the work for you.
- Your best tool is your sponsor.

Nancy's Favorites

- Don't work hard for a living; work smart for a lifestyle.
- Money isn't everything, but it sure keeps you in touch with the kids and grandkids.

- What you do today will determine your future.
- The time for women is now.
- Why isn't everyone in Network Marketing?
- Better in the morning to be able to roll over than to roll out when the alarm goes off.
- You can be there to see your children grow up.
- It's all about fun, happiness and a healthy lifestyle.
- Times are always changing and it's good to learn new things.
- Your dreams can come true if you get the vision of Network Marketing.
- You never know when you are going to meet your next best friend or get your next best idea.
- You either want to own your life or you don't, it's your choice.
- Network Marketing is a paid social life.
- Do something fun every day.
- Lifestyle is something everyone wants to have and you can have it!
- I have never met a man who doesn't like working with a woman, especially if she is making him money.
- Your journey in life is about the choices you have made.
- Life is like a book, if you don't travel you only read one page.
- Take back your vacation/holiday.
- A good attitude can make a huge difference.
- You can make it in Network Marketing if you use the tools and never give up.
- What would your life look like if time and money were not a problem?
- Network Marketing is the greatest gift you can give a friend.
- You can create a second income without a second job.
- Time is our most precious and limited resource.
- If you really want something, you can make it in Network Marketing.

- Some people travel in their mind, some people travel in their heart, and some people actually go somewhere.
- Women are the best because they have the nature to nurture.
- You are never too old to get started.
- Experience is your best teacher.
- There is no substitute for experience.
- What is the joy in your life?
- Think smart, build smart, be smart.
- Choose to be happy and positive.
- Fun to be free.
- Welcome to freedom.
- Why keep working for a living when you can work for a lifestyle and really make a difference.
- Stress is the number one killer.
- We're in the people business; we change people's lives one person at a time.
- Keep it simple, make it fun and people will want to join you.
- Don't take yourself so seriously. Lighten up and have fun.
- The more fun you have, the more successful you will be.
- In Networking, you have more fun per hour.
- Having fun is your full time business.
- There are a lot of lonely people that should join a Networking company.
- Be a good listener.
- There is a light at the end of the tunnel.
- Learn to ask questions.
- You are not going to get out of this world alive so you might as well go for it.
- One life, live it.
- One life, own it.

- Almost everyone would like to travel.
- Cruising is good for the soul.
- Shopping is a good thing.
- Living on a budget is malo (Spanish for bad).

Don & Nancy's Favorites

- Are you sick and tired of being sick and tired?
- We are not on vacation, this is how we live.
- Breaking the home barrier is being at home wherever you are.
- We ate at sixty-five Chart House restaurants in eighteen months and received two sets of tickets to fly around the world free.
- We are lifestyle trainers and we teach people how to have a better life.
- Without time, money and your health, you really don't have much of a life.
- The audio version of the *45 Second Presentation* book is for people who can't read, don't like to read, don't have time to read, or are blind.
- The power of one is huge.
- Children can be great motivators.
- International travel: only take what you can carry yourself.
- Mistakes can cost you time and money.
- Timing is very important.
- Listening is more important than talking.
- We like to teach our people that anyone can do The System.
- Traveling with a purpose is better than traveling as a tourist.
- Wear the Own Your Life pin every day.
- We travel so much our whole life is a write-off.
- We chose Richard Rabbit as our mascot because rabbits multiply so fast.
- Having The System will make you confident.

APPENDIX:
Tools to Implement The System

As discussed there are a number of tools that will help you become successful as you implement The System. You can either do what we did, spend 43 years figuring out The System and developing tools to help you build; or you can take advantage of the tools that are in place already so you can start building your organization today. Below are a list of tools that we talked about in this book and where you can get them. In addition we have listed out some of our other training material that we thought you would be interested in.

30th Anniversary Edition – The 45 Second Presentation That Will Change Your Life –

Go to www.45SecondTools.com. This edition also includes a bonus disc of "How To Build Your Business Using The 45 Second Presentation which is basically this book on CD.

Audio Book - 30th Anniversary Edition – The 45 Second Presentation That Will Change Your Life –

This revised 4 Disc plus diagram book set has been completely updated with the new chapters and includes a bonus disc by Nancy Failla. To purchase visit: www.45SecondTools.com.

Own Your Life (Lapel Pin)

Available at www.45SecondTools.com. The popular Own Your Life lapel pin is a perfect way to stimulate conversation. Show others that you "Own Your Life" and they just may be curious as to how to own their life! This pin is perfect for giving out to your downline or new recruits.

Lifestyle Business Cards

Lifestyle business cards are custom business cards that have the 45 Second Presentation printed on the back with absolutely no company information on the card. This is an essential tool for completing Step 1 of The System. You can choose to have them printed wherever you like, however, at www.45SecondTools.com there are a number of options that we like and they are ready to print.

SAVE 20% on your first order of lifestyle business cards by entering the promo code: LIFE1ST at checkout.

IOwnMyLife.net

This replicated website acts as a bridge between your cold and warm market as explained previously. In addition there are great training and other video presentations that you can send your warm market or your downline. It is a must have to properly implement The System. If you are curious as to what they look like…just visit ours at www.IOwnMyLife.net/donandnancy or www.donandnancyfailla.com. To get your site set up visit: www.IOwnMyLife.net and click on the "Join IOwnMyLife" button on the top of the page.

The Napkin Presentation DVD

Now you can show the famous Napkin Presentations in DVD format right from your living room. Use it with your prospects to help "teach them to drive" before introducing your vehicle. As an added BONUS, this disc also has my famous presentation on The System. So you can teach it to others in less than 10 minutes from your home...no speaking fee required.

The 45 Second Presentation Pass-Out Cards

Use these convenient cards as a substitute to the lifestyle business cards. It also has The 45 Second Presentation printed on it, but also demonstrates the power of networking by showing interest income vs. residual income. Great for Step 1 of The System

Just The FAQs About Network Marketing: Straight Answers To Frequently Asked Questions About Networking

Whether you are just starting out or have been in the industry for 10 years, you can still benefit from the over 36 years of experience of Don and Nancy Failla. While it serves as a fundamental guide for the advanced distributor, this book can double as a powerful prospecting piece, introducing your prospects to the business of Network Marketing, and ultimately financial freedom.

Host a Meeting with Don & Nancy Failla

To schedule a time to have Don & Nancy come and teach your group The System and customize a presentation for your group contact Sound Concepts at 888.285.6317

Customization

To customize this book or any of Don & Nancy's tools, please contact Sound Concepts at 888.285.6317.

ABOUT THE AUTHOR

Don Failla has been involved in the Network Marketing industry for over 40 years. During that time, many have noticed the trademark Hawaiian style shirts that he constantly wears. While vacationing in Hawaii a number of years back, Don bought a shirt, and while wearing it, had a pleasant, relaxed and fun-filled stay. He then realized that he wanted to feel that relaxed and content for the rest of his life. This attitude has pushed Don to help thousands of others achieve the same lifestyle.

How has he accomplished that? His System, *The 45 Second Presentation That Will Change Your Life*, has been incorporated into various publications, audio/video presentations and seminars, all of which are regularly used in countries throughout the world. His publications truly are international bestsellers.

Beginning his networking career in 1967, Don, like most network marketers, experienced success as well as failure. However, he keenly observed those factors that seemed to be effective in building a large organization. Incorporating what he learned, Don eventually developed the simple yet highly effective "napkin presentations" and incorporated them as the core of his "45 Second" program. The book has become the networking Bible, with over 5 million copies sold, and translated into 20 languages. Don's proven success (more than 800,000 distributors in his group in only 17 years), as well as his simple, straightforward style has led to the remarkable success of hundreds of thousands of network marketers throughout the world.

Today, Don and his wife Nancy travel the globe teaching their System as International Network Trainers.

Made in the USA
Charleston, SC
22 May 2013